MW00676142

Firestone

A Legend. A Century. A Celebration.™

By Paul Dickson and William D. Hickman

Edited by Nelson Eddy

Published in 2000 by
Forbes Custom Publishing
60 Fifth Avenue
New York, NY 10011

Library of Congress Cataloging-in-Publication Data

Dickson, Paul.
Firestone: a legend, a century, a celebration, 1900-2000 / by Paul Dickson and William D. Hickman.
p. cm.
Includes bibliographical references and index.
ISBN 0-8281-1338-6 (alk. paper)
1. Firestone, Harvey Samuel, 1868-1938. 2. Industrialists--United States--Biography.
3. Firestone Tire and Rubber Company--History. 4. Tire industry--United
States--History. 5. Rubber industry and trade--United States--History. I. Hickman,
William. II. Title.

HD9161.5.T572 F573 1999
338.7'6782'092--dc21
[B]

99-0052691

Printed in the United States of America

CONTENTS

William Clay Ford, Jr.

I never met Harvey S. Firestone or Henry Ford. My famous great-grandfathers died long before I was born. But I grew up with a deep understanding of both men from history books and family lore. Of the many stories told over the years about Harvey Firestone and Henry Ford, what impressed me most was that each considered his business a family business first and foremost, and everyone who worked for them was a family member.

Harvey S. Firestone groomed his sons to succeed him in running the company. All five became members of the board of directors. Two sons, Raymond and my grandfather, Harvey S. Firestone, Jr., became chairman and chief executive officer at various points in the company's history.

My grandfather and his brothers literally grew up in the tire business. As children, they toured factories and took part in countless company events. In fact, my grandfather was still a child when he was designated the official company representative to "open" Firestone's first plant. He pulled the switch that started the production line in Akron, Ohio.

Firestone thrived, in large part, because of this deep sense of family. Much like Ford Motor Company, this set The Firestone Tire & Rubber Company apart from all its competitors and gave it a unique personality.

But neither Ford nor Firestone would have had such a lasting impact on the world without their founders' total commitment to the notion of personal mobility.

For Harvey S. Firestone, that meant creating new markets for his tire business beyond the automobile. He expanded his company into over-the-highway truck transportation, farm equipment and into markets around the world. It also meant choosing his battles, such as when he opposed the British rubber cartels by establishing his Liberian rubber plantation.

For Henry Ford, it meant providing affordable mass transportation. Before the Model T, most Americans had never ventured more than 20 miles away from home in their entire lives. Together with his friend Harvey S. Firestone, they gave generations of Americans the mobility to work, live, travel and play where they wanted.

In addition to their business relationship, my great-grandfathers were close friends. They were among the group known as the vagabonds, which also included Thomas Edison and John Burroughs. My maternal grandparents Elizabeth and Harvey S. Firestone, Jr., were lucky enough to spend time with the group on some of its famous camping trips in the early '20s. One of my favorite stories is how Thomas Edison made sure the group had comfortable lighting in the woods as he always packed a generator.

I am privileged to have had two American icons as my great-grandfathers. Their legacies have inspired me to contribute what I can to industry and to society as we enter a new century. I look forward to building on the legacies they began nearly 100 years ago. I believe that both my great-grandfathers would be proud of how their ideas have flourished.

William Clay Ford, Jr.

EDITOR'S NOTE: William Clay Ford, Jr., is chairman of the board of Ford Motor Company. He is the son of Martha Firestone and William Clay Ford; grandson of Harvey S. Firestone, Jr., and Edsel Ford, and great-grandson of Harvey S. Firestone, Sr., and Henry Ford.

BEST TODAY...
STILL BETTER
TOMORROW
Non
Skid
Tires
FIRESTONE TIRE & RUBBER CO.
RUBBER TIRES FOR VEHICLES AND AUTOMOBILES
NEW YORK, N. Y.
704-727
WEST VIRGINIA

CHAPTER 1

A CENTURY IN THE MAKING

1

Plows, patent medicines, racing ponies and Firestone's rural roots

The turn of the century. Perhaps we place undo importance on the inevitable close of the 20th century. After all, there is no audible click as some great cosmic odometer changes to the next millennium. However, as we enter the new century let us pause on our increasingly harried journey, to take this rare opportunity to see how far we've come as a world and in what direction we've traveled.

Three of the 20th Century's greatest minds and lifelong friends, Henry Ford, Thomas Edison and Harvey S. Firestone, photographed in what would be their last meeting at Edison's laboratory in Ft. Myers, Florida, in March of 1931. (Russ Vitale Photography)

Advancements in society, science, culture, and economic conditions are all marvelous methods for gauging our forward progress. This pictorial history brings together each of these elements in the measure of a single company with the familiar name—a company called Firestone.

Firestone is a perfect reflection of the 20th century. Not simply because it began with, and successfully spanned the century we celebrate, but also because the name Firestone is tied to many of the major events and themes that have defined the last 100 years. Firestone was a powerful presence—moving us from the farm to the factory as we ushered in the 20th century; keeping us rolling during the Age of Invention and the dawn of the automobile; helping us ride out the Great Depression; equipping us for two world wars, and conflicts in Korea and Vietnam, in an effort to overcome the conflicts that divide the globe; leading public campaigns that helped build our interstate highway system and created the long-distance trucking industry; helping to propel us into space; pioneering sports marketing and the power of public relations with an unequaled record of 50 Indy 500® victories; elevating the art of advertising through corporate-sponsored programming such as the *Voice of Firestone;* and, finally, testing the real potential of the global marketplace as the company prepared for the next century with the international merger between Firestone and Bridgestone.

At every turn, Firestone was there.

"Firestone, Edison and Ford were largely responsible for jerking the world out of its horse-and-buggy pace and thrusting it into the era of speed."

– Chicago American, 1938

A master at taking his message to the people, Harvey S. Firestone bolstered the fledgling American trucking industry at the close of World War I with the "Ship by Truck" movement. (Bridgestone/Firestone Collection)

The long road, however, hasn't been without its challenges—disruptions due to labor and management concerns, political intrigue and unrest overseas, a historic product recall, and the threat of global competition. In each case, Firestone has sought to emerge a better business, striving, as its founder urged, to be "the best today, still better tomorrow."

As the company stands today, there is reason to believe it is living up to its promise. Firestone is one of a revered class of internationally known brands that continues to thrive. From a company of a dozen people crafting carriage tires, it has grown to become an icon, one of the world's largest rubber and tire manufacturers, a $7.4-billion international enterprise of 45,000 individuals at 40 production facilities in the Western Hemisphere producing more than 100 million tires a year as well as numerous diversified products. There are many reasons to celebrate.

This centennial album is more than a record of Firestone's many milestones. It is a celebration of the company and the incredible century its journey encompasses. It is not meant to be a complete reference nor an exhaustive study of Firestone history. Instead, it is a quick and celebratory trip through the 20th century from the unique perspective of a company whose journey parallels the major events of the world around it. It is a trip that is purposefully heavy on scenery, rather than straight history, richly illustrated with the most extensive collection of Firestone photographs ever published in a single place. Note, too, the route you'll be taking is topical rather than chronological, to speed you to your desired destination, whether it be more information on motorsports or the successful merger with Bridgestone. Those who prefer a more traditional route will find the history of the company conveniently mapped in a detailed timeline at the end of the book.

Now that we've given you the keys, it's time to get started.

In 1911, tires are crafted by hand at the Firestone tire building room. Using crude production lines, the tire is created around a mold in much the same way a shoemaker crafts a shoe around a last. (Bridgestone/Firestone Collection)

The Firestone name has long been synonymous with champions, as this series of ads from the 1940s suggests. (Bridgestone/Firestone Collection)

The dedication to quality and superior products, a cornerstone of The Firestone Tire & Rubber Company, is the driving force in modern day tire and non-tire production plants. (Bridgestone/Firestone Collection)

From Horses to Horsepower

At the turn of the century, America was still in its innocence, a vast expanse of small towns and farms. Six of every ten citizens lived outside the glow of city lights. Even though

Akron, Ohio, just after the turn of the century, as depicted in a postcard. The "rubber barons" were establishing themselves in this boomtown and, as Harvey S. Firestone noted, "I cannot say that the new tire company was particularly welcome in Akron." (Bridgestone/Firestone Collection)

America was in the middle of an unprecedented period of discovery known as the Age of Invention, the kerosene lamp, the outhouse and the horse-drawn carriage were still the standards of rural life. A great change lay just down the road.

OHIO
HISTORICAL MARKER
FIRESTONE HOMESTEAD
1828
Birthplace on December 20, 1868, of Harvey S. Firestone, founder of The Firestone Tire and Rubber Company. One of the first brick houses in Columbiana County, it was built in 1828 by Harvey S. Firestone's great-grandfather, Nicholas Firestone, who acquired title to 640 acres in 1804 by a land grant signed by Thomas Jefferson, President of the United States, and James Madison, Secretary of State.
1968 THE OHIO HISTORICAL SOCIETY 6-15

Harvey S. Firestone's roots in rural America are commemorated in this historic marker placed by the Ohio Historical Society at the Firestone Homestead in Columbiana. (Modern Tire Dealer Archives)

The world came slowly sauntering into the 20th century harnessed to a horse, but the spinning rubber wheels of an automobile would speed it into the future. At the time Harvey S. Firestone entered the race, America's sparse population of 76 million was still served by more than 20 million horses. Only 8,000 registered automobiles sputtered and bounced over the roadways. By 1915, that number exploded to 2.5 million with a half-million new passenger cars sold each year. By 1928, the country boasted more automobiles than telephones.

America was a country that associated freedom and prosperity with movement. Hadn't our forefathers first moved to the shores of the New World to find freedom and economic opportunity?

Once here, the search for greater shares of the two quickly moved us from East to West. Now a new invention—the automobile—priced by Henry Ford for the masses, offered to free us from the confining shackles of a train schedule. We could move whenever and wherever we wanted at will. The car redefined our character as a country. Freedom, individuality, and the American penchant for spontaneity were all accelerated by the automobile. Soon motels and shopping centers became common roadside scenery. The automobile made popular the notion of buying on credit. It embodied the spirit of invention, and was continually rolled out in ever new and improved models. It created the tourism industry, and fueled movies, books, and songs as well as firing the appetite for adventure and the need for more national parks.

Like most Americans, fresh from the farm and aboard a horse and carriage, Harvey S. Firestone rode into the very center of this great swirl of activity. As biographer James C. Young put it: "[Firestone] stood at the crossroads of what had been and what would be."

But let's not put the cart before the horse. Let's go back to the farm where this story and the turn of the century began.

Rolling off the Farm

Harvey S. Firestone was born on a farm near Columbiana, Ohio, on December 20, 1868. Located in the eastern part of the state, the Firestone farm was started as a homestead by

Harvey S. Firestone, at his desk. Though his company was renowned for the development of many innovations including mechanically fastened straight-side tires, demountable rims, the non-skid tread, cord fabric, gum-dipping and balloon tires, Firestone's greatest achievements were as a businessman and marketing genius. **(Russ Vitale Photography)**

Harvey's great grandfather, Nicholas, in 1797. In 1804, it was expanded by 640 acres through a land grant deeded to him by President Thomas Jefferson. Harvey S. Firestone grew up in what's believed to be Ohio's first brick home, a nine-room residence completed in 1828. The hardship of working the land would sow in the young Firestone seeds of strength, independence and a penchant for hard work that served as the backbone of his later success.

After graduation from Columbiana High School and completion of an advanced business course, Firestone began his career, not as an inventor, but as a businessman. Although he later led a company known for its many innovations, it was as a businessman—an individual skilled in the art of recognizing society's needs, bringing to market a product that served those needs, and communicating that fact to the marketplace in convincing fashion—that Firestone truly excelled.

The Firestone Homestead in Columbiana, Ohio, was built in 1828, crafted from homemade bricks created from clay found on the farm.
(University of Akron Archives – Firestone Collection)

Firestone's first stop as businessman was short-lived. He took a bookkeeping job at a coal company in Columbus, Ohio, on the first of January, 1888. His employer quickly went out of business. Moving on, he became a salesman for a company whose line of goods included patent medicines and flavoring extracts. At first, the man who would sell his ideas to the world's leaders, entertain leading actors, and become the voice of culture throughout the country, experienced a bit of stage fright when calling on customers. Although he conquered his fear, he never became completely comfortable with his new line of work. He was troubled by the claims made by the makers of the patent medicines he was asked to sell.

"I made up my mind right there," Firestone told an early biographer, "that I never would present anything for sale unless I absolutely knew it was honest and according to specifications."

Though he continued with the company, he sold only extracts—products he was confident worked as promised—until this company, too, unexpectedly went out of business. Although out of a job, a guiding principle in his life was established—honesty and quality above everything else.

Like most young Americans in the decade before the turn of the century, Firestone looked to the promise of the big city for work. His next stop was Detroit. Here he hitched his dreams to a horse and buggy.

The Wheels Begin Turning

In the 1890s, before being recognized around the world as the Motor City, Detroit was the hotbed of the horse and buggy. The city's fashionable young men loved to race along Woodward Avenue and the Boulevard, showing off the power and beauty of their horse-drawn carriages. The right horse was important to the outcome of a race, but so was hitching that horsepower to the right buggy. Every detail was important, right down to the wheels. Firestone used the popularity of racing as a sales vehicle in his new line of work. He took a job as a sales agent for the Columbus Buggy Works and began winning races to showcase the quality of the product. Shortly after he arrived in Detroit, the city welcomed

one of the first new rubber-tired racing buggies from England. Firestone was among the first to own one of the new vehicles and was soon winning hotly contested street races.

Firestone's inner fire for racing is noteworthy. It was a sharp business move that would later dramatically place his company ahead of the competition at Indy. In his book *Men and Rubber,* Firestone recalls an incident from his early days as a racer that offers insight on his personal daring, eye for quality and performance, his power to instill confidence and, finally, the great ingenuity he showed when it came to trotting out his new discovery to market.

"My greatest triumph was with a big, wild sort of horse that had great speed but simply would not race. Either he would not start, or somewhere in the race he would go wild and cut up. I thought he was not being handled rightly, and the owner gave him to me to race. The whole thing was to get that horse's confidence, and after weeks of effort I got it; he came to believe that nothing could happen to him if I were driving. I tried him out behind a buggy on the Boulevard and he was able to pass anything. Then I entered him in a gentlemen's race on a private mile track near Detroit. The entry was taken as a joke and I made no pretense it was other than a joke, for I was afraid he would get cold feet in the race—as he always did. Still, I took a chance. There were four or five horses in the race and in the first heat I kept my horse back, just letting him trail along and giving him no chance at all to get nervous. I used that heat merely as a practice spin to show him that he really had nothing to fear. In the second heat, having more confidence, he started without difficulty, but I kept him until the stretch; then I let him go and he won. The crowd was all up for the third heat—it was two out

Harvey S. Firestone in his buggy at the Grosse Point, Michigan, race track in 1893. This vehicle was the first equipped with solid rubber tires in the Detroit area.
(Bridgestone/Firestone Collection)

You Can Take the Boy Out of the Country, But...

Roots are important. Without a doubt, Harvey S. Firestone's country upbringing ingrained in him the values, insights, and invaluable experience he harvested later in his big city success.

The farm was never far from Firestone's mind. When business seemed too demanding, he returned to the farm for renewal.

"It helps me to think, when I go down to the old homestead at Columbiana," Firestone said.

He also returned the favor by bringing renewal and his own rich harvest of new ideas to the farm. Firestone personally experimented with the first practical pneumatic tractor tire—and did it in the straw hat and big overalls he loved to wear.

When the company staged its breathtaking displays at the great world's fairs and expositions of the 1930s—the Century of Progress in Chicago, the Great Lakes Exposition in Cleveland, and the New York World's Fair of 1939–40—the Firestone exhibit always looked to the future while showcasing the farm.

Years after its founder's death, the Firestone company restored his farmhouse as the centerpiece of the 1,200-acre Firestone Homestead and Test Center. Today the primary testing facility for the company's farm tires is still located in the same Ohio town where he toiled as a boy and first became interested in making farm life easier for others.

(Henry Ford Museum & Greenfield Village)

"To me," he said, "the American farm represents the spirit and fundamentals that have made America so great as a nation..."

Being reared on a farm was an experience Firestone shared with most of the young people of his generation, along with his lifelong friend, Henry Ford. Ford, too, understood the dramatic impact his products had on rural life. He watched as his horseless carriage carried young people away from their roots in increasing numbers. Like Firestone, Ford tried to give something of himself back to the farm with the invention of new tractors and equipment. With the creation and endowment of Greenfield Village in Dearborn, Michigan, he even tried to preserve a small piece of 19th-century life and the way things were before the coming of the automobile.

In 1985, Firestone's sons moved the family's original farmhouse and buildings to Greenfield Village as a tribute to Firestone's development of rubber farm tires and other agricultural improvements. It also served as a poignant reminder of the roots of Firestone and Ford's friendship.

Today, because of Harvey S. Firestone's leadership, the company still enjoys a leading share of the agricultural tire business. In Greenfield Village, more than one million visitors annually explore the Firestone Farmstead to witness life on a working 19th-century farm and to see just how far Firestone's tires have taken us.

of three—every man in the race was wealthy except me, and the crowd was rooting for me.

"Going to the start was the biggest thrill I ever had. I had wanted to trail in that heat and then go ahead in the stretch, but I had the pole position, and if I let the bunch get far ahead, I would have to go completely around them in the stretch. On the other hand, I was afraid that if my horse cut ahead too soon he would think there was nothing more to work for and decide to stop running. I compromised by holding him back just enough to prevent the next horse from taking the pole away from us and as we came into the stretch I let him go for all he was worth. And go he did! He went so fast and true that we won that race by at least three or four lengths."

Besides realizing racing's power to sell and noting the superior performance of rubber tires, Firestone made another important discovery during his days in Detroit with the Columbus Buggy Works. He made a chance acquaintance with a young man and sold him a buggy tire that propelled the two of them into history.

The tire was a new pneumatic, air-filled invention. The acquaintance would become a life-long friend. His name was Henry Ford.

Henry Ford and Harvey S. Firestone were two powerful captains of industry who genuinely enjoyed each other's company. Here they chat by the fence at the May 29, 1932 Indianapolis 500, won by Fred Frame on Firestone tires.

(University of Akron Archives–Firestone Collection)

FIRESTONE TIRE & RUBBER CO.
MANUFACTURERS OF
RUBBER TIRES
FOR VEHICLES & AUTOMOBILES.
UNITED STATES AMERICA
To all to whom these presents shall come
Whereas
has presented to the Commissioner of Patents a petition praying
for the grant of Letters Patent for an alleged new and useful improvement in
a description of which invention is contained in the Specification of which
a copy is hereunto annexed and made a part hereof, and has complied
with the various requirements of Law in such cases made and provided, and
Whereas upon due examination made the said Claimant is adjudged
to be justly entitled to a Patent under the Law.
Now therefore these Letters Patent are to grant unto the said
heirs or assigns
for the term of Seventeen years from the
day
one thousand nine hundred
the exclusive right to make, use and vend the said invention throughout
United States and the Territories thereof.
In testimony whereof I have hereunto
and caused the seal of the Patent
affixed at the City of
the year of our Lord one thousand
Independence of the United States
FIRESTONE TIRE & RUBBER COMPANY
"Firestone"
AKRON, OHIO, U.S.A.
irestone Park
PRES CHURCH

CHAPTER 2

FAST FRIENDS

2

Connecting rubber to rims, four remarkable friends and an American adventure along the road

It may have been the defining moment of the coming century and the Firestone company—that incredible instant when a young Henry Ford walked into the Columbus Buggy Works and asked the young Harvey Firestone for a tire.

"The first time I met Harvey Firestone he was an agent for the Columbus Buggy Works in Detroit," Ford later recalled. "That was in 1895. At the time I

"The 75th anniversary of The Firestone Tire & Rubber Company is a time to reflect on what has made this a great and successful company. What I think it comes down to is people working together."

– Raymond C. Firestone, chairman, writing to the employees on the company's anniversary, August 3, 1975

was building my first automobile. It was about complete, and I was using bicycle tires. The car weighed 500 pounds, which was too much for the light tires. I went in the buggy works to see about obtaining some solid rubber tires as a substitute. Firestone told me he had just received new tires, that were a great deal softer, on a buggy being unpacked in the rear. They were pneumatic tires and I had him order me a set."

The rest, as they say, is history—the history of the 20th century.

The meeting set the wheels in motion, propelling the automobile down the road and Firestone into the tire business. And the pneumatic tire was key to the success of both. Although a solid rubber tire was superior to a metal wheel, it still had virtually no give. When driven at anything but the slowest speeds, an automobile on hard rubber tires was literally shaken to pieces—along with its passenger. But pneumatic tires transported automobile and passenger on a comfortable cushion of air. The tire's inner tube contained air under pressure while the tire's outer casing (the tire itself) protected the inner tube and endured the wear of carrying a heavy vehicle over all types of roads.

Without the pneumatic tire, which first saw widespread use with the bicycle, the development of the automobile would likely have been delayed.

From that first casual meeting between Firestone and Ford that ushered in the turn of the century to the monumental merger of Bridgestone and Firestone that welcomed the

When Henry Ford purchased 2,000 sets of pneumatic tires from Harvey S. Firestone, in 1906, that order and others that followed were a source of pride to the fledgling tire company. Here, a shipment on June 16, 1906, is loaded onto a well-marked rail car.

(Bridgestone/Firestone Collection)

The plant at Miller and Sweitzer Avenues as it looked in 1911. The plant housed the Rim Division until Firestone Steel Products plants were built later.

(Modern Tire Dealer Archives)

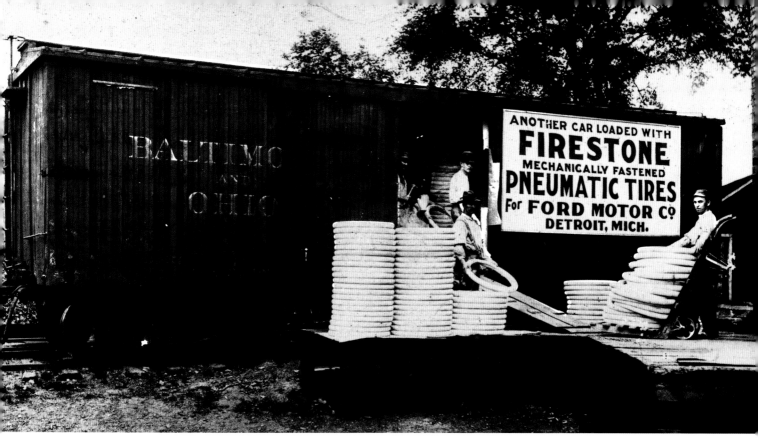

new millennium, powerful relationships would play a pivotal role in the life of the company.

A thoughtful student of the marketplace, Firestone saw a future in tires. In 1896, with just $1,000 to his name, he moved to Chicago to sell rubber carriage tires. But he never forgot his meeting with Henry Ford.

By 1900, he was convinced the horse and carriage were on the way out and a new era—the Automobile Age—was beginning. Firestone was driven to be a part of the new movement. And to be at the very hub and heart of the industry, in terms of tires, meant moving to Akron, Ohio.

Akron was the place where natural latex from around the world was made into tires and other rubber items. It was called "the Rubber Capital of the World," known for its "Rubber Barons." Firestone would quickly take his place among the city's manufacturing elite.

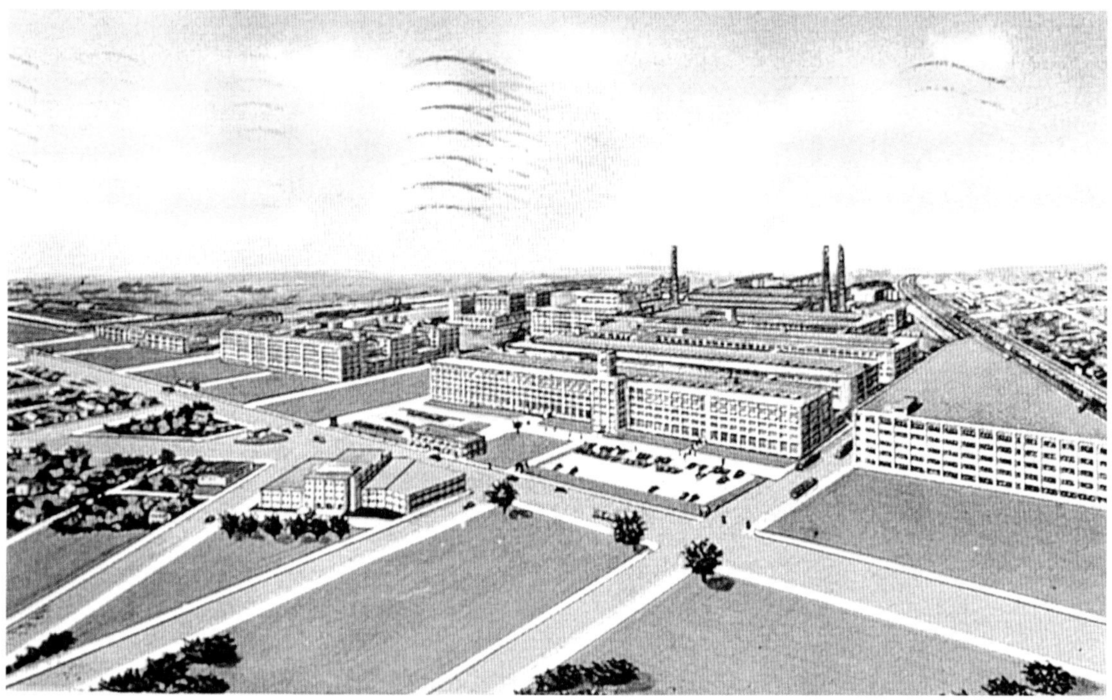

This view of the The Firestone Tire & Rubber Company decorated postcards during the late 1920s.
(Bridgestone/Firestone Collection)

The labor-intensive art of building a tire (circa 1911) required the rubber be washed, dried, milled, compounded and cut. By 1915, tire-building machines would be added to the manufacturing process, resulting in a better product, made more efficiently.
(Bridgestone/Firestone Collection)

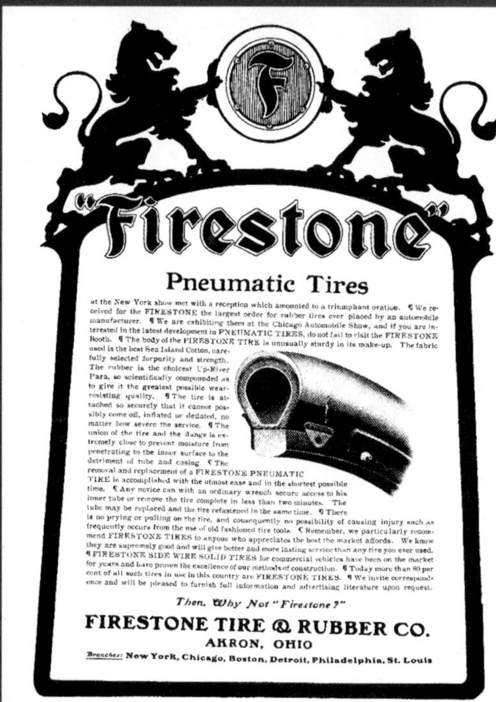

"Firestone"
Pneumatic Tires
at the New York show met with a reception which amounted to a triumphant ovation. ¶ We received for the FIRESTONE the largest order for rubber tires ever placed by an automobile manufacturer. ¶ We are exhibiting them at the Chicago Automobile Show, and if you are interested in the latest development in PNEUMATIC TIRES, do not fail to visit the FIRESTONE Booth. ¶ The body of the FIRESTONE TIRE is unusually sturdy in its make-up. The fabric used is the best Sea Island Cotton, carefully selected forpurity and strength. The rubber is the choicest Up-River Para, so scientifically compounded as to give it the greatest possible wear-resisting quality. ¶ The tire is attached so securely that it cannot possibly come off, inflated or deflated, no matter how severe the service. ¶ The union of the tire and the flange is extremely close to prevent moisture from penetrating to the inner surface to the detriment of tube and casing. ¶ The removal and replacement of a FIRESTONE PNEUMATIC TIRE is accomplished with the utmost ease and in the shortest possible time. ¶ Any novice can with an ordinary wrench secure access to his inner tube or remove the tire complete in less than two minutes. The tube may be replaced and the tire refastened in the same time. ¶ There is no prying or pulling on the tire, and consequently no possibility of causing injury such as frequently occurs from the use of old fashioned tire tools. ¶ Remember, we particularly recommend FIRESTONE TIRES to anyone who appreciates the best the market affords. We know they are supremely good and will give better and more lasting service than any tire you ever used. ¶ FIRESTONE SIDE WIRE SOLID TIRES for commercial vehicles have been on the market for years and have proven the excellence of our methods of construction. ¶ Today more than 80 per cent of all such tires in use in this country are FIRESTONE TIRES. ¶ We invite correspondence and will be pleased to furnish full information and advertising literature upon request.
Then, Why Not "Firestone?"
FIRESTONE TIRE & RUBBER CO.
AKRON, OHIO
Branches: New York, Chicago, Boston, Detroit, Philadelphia, St. Louis

Early Firestone advertising highlights the ease of changing a pneumatic tire, a popular innovation for which the tire and rubber company was highly regarded.
(Modern Tire Dealer Archives)

On August 3, 1900, Harvey S. Firestone started The Firestone Tire & Rubber Company in Akron. He rolled into town already behind. Dr. Benjamin Franklin Goodrich, who brought his tire factory to Akron in 1870, was credited with making the first pneumatic automobile tires. Brothers Frank and Charlie Seiberling started the Goodyear Tire & Rubber Company in 1898, two years prior to Firestone's arrival.

The fledgling Firestone company got off to a slow start, losing a little money during each of its first two years. Firestone knew why. He was buying his tires from competitors instead of making and selling his own. This arrangement left no room in the price to make a profit. He would have to make his own tires or go out of business. Along with making a profit, the decision allowed him to control the product's quality—something he'd wanted to do since his patent medicine days.

A Ford in His Future

Firestone's first factory opened in 1902. It employed 12 men and was housed in a small, abandoned building—a dilapidated foundry. Firestone bought the vacant workplace with a $4,500 loan from the bank that owned it. The factory's machinery was all secondhand. From these humble beginnings, the company rose to prosperity in three short years. Once again, Firestone's turn of fortune revolved around a relationship.

"A few years after our first meeting, Firestone entered business for himself," Henry Ford recalled. "He was the first tire manufacturer to seek an order from us in 1906. He got the order—2,000 sets of detachable tires—and he has furnished us with about half of our tires since."

Along with his insistence on quality, Firestone had both a salesman's knack for nurturing relationships and a savvy marketer's eye for giving people what they needed. It proved a powerful combination.

"Firestone, in 1904, came up with the precursor of the modern tire—a mechanically fastened, straight-sided, automobile pneumatic," Stewart Steiner wrote in his unpublished history of the company. "It overcame the danger of flopping off the wheel and it was designed to replace the clincher, an exasperating creation that required a crowbar, muscular effort, and the patience of a saint to manipulate its hooked head of hard rubber into the under-cut rim. This was followed with a sequel called the universal rim that would accommodate either a straight side or a clincher, whichever the car manufacturer preferred."

By 1906, the company's sales passed the million-dollar mark and by the end of the century's first decade, Firestone was a name known nationally. The company raced to keep pace with car makers' demands for more and more tires—the industry ballooned from 2.4 million tires in 1910 to 37 million in 1920. Not only did the demand for tires increase, but heavier, faster cars also required stronger, more heat-resistant tires. The adept Firestone knew the importance of responding quickly to people's needs.

As important to the early success of the company as the customer relationships he was building, was the loyalty Firestone forged with his employees. In 1916, he introduced the company to the eight-hour workday and provided a thousand acres in South Akron to build Firestone Park, a much-needed residential community for workers in a booming Rubber City that was growing faster than any other city in the country. To help a city expanding from 69,000 to 208,000 citizens in just five years, he built schools, churches, and offered financial assistance to employees buying homes.

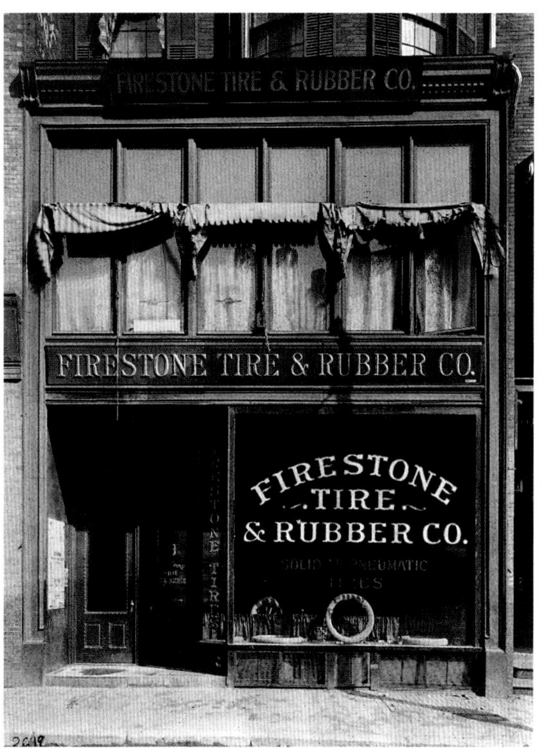

Early in its history, The Firestone Tire & Rubber Company became a familiar fixture on the American main street. In this classic downtown store, the Firestone name is proudly displayed.

(Bridgestone/Firestone Collection)

Harvey S. Firestone was becoming more than just a manufacturer. He was becoming a national figure. His leadership extended beyond the reach of a rubber company to embrace the concerns of a country, the continent, and the world. In 1917, on the brink of world war, Firestone offered President Woodrow Wilson "the use of the factory organization and all facilities in any way that can be of service to the government at war."

Camping with Greatness

Imagine today that Bill Gates, Michael Dell, Warren Buffett, and Jane Goodall—four of the pre-eminent minds in innovation, technology, business, and the environment—have assembled themselves, not for a symposium, but to take an extended vacation. Together. They'd be camping across the country. The trip would be inundated with media coverage. Not only would the day-by-day details and descriptions of their journey fill the headlines, they'd capture our imagination and fill our conversations. Think of the celebrities as well as throngs of everyday people greeting them at every turn. Perhaps even the President would make an appearance.

For Harvey S. Firestone, business was his pleasure. He used the highly publicized road trips with his famous friends to test his tires and popularize the novel notion of auto touring. Here, he stops to check his company's workmanship during a 1923 camping trip.
(Bridgestone/Firestone Collection)

As fantastic as it sounds, trips such as these were taken more than three-quarters of a century ago. And their effect was no less astonishing to the media, society, and general public of the day. Starting in 1916, Thomas A. Edison, the most prolific inventor of all time; Henry Ford, creator of the world's first popular motorcar and the modern assembly line; John Burroughs, one of the country's earliest environmentalists; and Harvey S. Firestone, creator of an industrial empire based on innovative management that crafted and marketed quality rubber products, traveled on a series of camping trips across the country.

So popular were their adventures together that two U.S. presidents—Warren G. Harding and Calvin Coolidge—joined them on parts of their journey.

The American public loved the spectacle, causing one biographer to write, "Their vagabondage struck a human note." While the public might not relate to the wealth, prestige, and privilege of the campers, they could understand the need to get away from it all, to escape from the complex civilization they had helped create. As Firestone biographer Alfred Lief wrote, "In truth, they were simple men on a fresh air holiday."

These "simple men" enjoyed the services of drivers and attendants to pitch their tents. They roughed it in the wild with the most modern conveniences including battery-powered lighting arranged by the man who enlightened the world, the great Edison. Ford's personal chef, Harold Sato of Japan, prepared meals.

The campers' meals were served from a car specially crafted by Ford. This amazing vehicle featured a furnished kitchen and pantry, a large gasoline stove fed by the car's gas tank, an icebox, and a rear panel that folded down into a table complete with a Lazy Susan and seating for 20. Travelers and guests were typically treated to a menu of broiled lamb chops, grilled ham, boiled potatoes, corn on the cob, hot biscuits, watermelon, and coffee.

Burroughs referred to Ford's movable feast as a "Waldorf-Astoria on wheels." While roughing it, the celebrated campers also traveled with a full-sized player piano and six thoroughbred horses.

While it would have been difficult for the campers not to have a good time given the conditions, the real treat was time spent together. As a privately published book by James C. Young, *Harvey Firestone*, observed, "No four men in the world ever were more congenial, and no other four could have had minds more diverse."

Burroughs was 79 years old when the trips began in 1916. This tall, thin figure with the flowing white beard was considered the nation's leading naturalist. His admirers included Walt Whitman and Theodore Roosevelt. A popular writer and poet, his work reflected a reverence for nature and urged its protection.

On August 21, 1918, the famed camping crew stops to mill around in the West Virginia mountains. Pictured, from left to right, are Thomas A. Edison, Harvey Firestone, Jr., John Burroughs, Henry Ford, and Harvey S. Firestone, Sr. Seated at the foot of the mill wheel is Professor R. J. H. DeLoach, a director of the Armour company and a friend of Burroughs and Firestone, Jr. (Modern Tire Dealer Archives)

Three of the driving forces of the 20th century – Ford, Edison, and Firestone – pause along the West Virginia roadside during their camping excursion in 1918. (Bridgestone/Firestone Collection)

Harvey S. Firestone and Thomas Edison check the map during a trip in 1924. The great American inventor served as the campers' navigator and often opted for dirt roads over the highway. (Bridgestone/Firestone Collection)

Interestingly, Burroughs had never driven a car until Ford gave him one as a gift. Then he was a reckless driver often seen in his native Ulster County, New York, driving "at high speed, his granddaughters clinging to each other and squealing as they bounced in the back seat." Ford shared Burroughs's love of nature and admired his writing. The auto magnate collected stones from Burroughs's farm in New York to build a bird fountain at his Greenfield Village museum in Dearborn, Michigan.

Edison was, perhaps, the most revered man in America at the time. At age 69 when the group took its first excursion, he was nearly deaf. Even though he relied on shouted conversations and written notes to communicate, Edison was named the navigator, riding in the lead car with compass in hand, choosing the route as they traveled. He preferred a dirt road to a highway and a small town to a large one.

While camping, Edison wore wrinkled clothing and seldom shaved or combed his hair. He was the wild and ragged picture of scientific genius. He considered those in the party who kept up appearances with barber shop shaves, "dudes and tenderfoots."

Firestone, the youngest of the campers at age 48 in 1916, stood in striking contrast to Edison. The short and slight but physically fit Firestone was a natty dresser who enjoyed living well. He regularly risked Edison's wrath, sneaking into town for a "city shave."

Firestone's chore during the rural adventures was to organize the logistics and look after everyone's comfort. He was also the camper most mindful of business interests. During the trips together, he often steered the caravan to the local Firestone store. The group quickly drew a crowd and photographs of the famous four filled the newspapers, often featuring "Firestone Tire & Rubber Company" signs in the background.

Travelers John Burroughs, Thomas Edison and Harvey S. Firestone wash away their early morning road-weariness near White Sulphur Springs, West Virginia, on August 6, 1918. (Bridgestone/Firestone Collection)

WITH FRIENDS LIKE THESE...

Perhaps the best way to measure the influence of the Firestone name on the culture and society of the 20th century is to take a peek at the people who made the pilgrimage to out-of-the-way Akron.

From Babe Ruth to Will Rogers, the great celebrities of the day came to call on Harvey S. Firestone. The whole family met classical music's great performers during the decades the *Voice of Firestone* played on radio and television. Dating back to the era of Gaston Chevrolet and Barney Oldfield, the family knew all the great race car drivers.

Every U.S. President from Wilson to Clinton has known one or more members of the Firestone family. Vice President Richard M. Nixon visited the Firestone Plantation in Liberia in 1957 and 1961. President John F. Kennedy presented Raymond C. Firestone with the Humanitarian Service Award of the Eleanor Roosevelt Cancer Foundation.

Harvey S. Firestone, President Calvin Coolidge, Henry Ford, Thomas Edison, Russell Firestone, Mrs. Coolidge, and Col. John Coolidge share a light moment at the Coolidge Homestead in Plymouth, Vermont, on August 19, 1924. The group is signing a sap bucket that will later commemorate this great meeting at the historic Wayside Inn.
(Bridgestone/Firestone Collection)

Even presidents-yet-to-be found inspiration in the presence of the Firestones. In 1919, Harvey S. Firestone, Sr., and Jr. sat down to a chicken dinner at the Firestone homestead in Columbiana with Lieutenant Colonel Dwight David Eisenhower—a meal and a meeting that planted in the future president the seeds for the interstate highway system during the Army Transcontinental Motor Convoy.

At Princeton University, Harvey S. Firestone, Jr., led the carefree life of a spirited college student. Appropriately, one of his good college friends, F. Scott Fitzgerald, captured the spirit of the Jazz Age in which the speed and style of motorcars figured so prominently. Harvey S. Firestone, Jr., was also privileged to accompany his father on some of his famed outings with Thomas Edison, Henry Ford, and John Burroughs.

"This was a very unique experience for me, a really wonderful thing," said the son. "Looking back, what I really got out of it was that I learned at a very early age that the great men like Edison were simple men, just as simple as can be. This made a very lasting impression on me and I noticed in later years that it was almost always true."

Leonard Firestone became involved in many ventures that partnered him with notable names. Jack Benny and George Burns joined him in buying a California grapefruit farm. He became part owner of the California Angels when the team joined the American Baseball league in 1961 as the Los Angeles Angels.

In the late 1970s, when the company was experiencing difficulties with its image, it needed a figure who could speak for Firestone with authority and credibility. An old college friend of Raymond Firestone came to the rescue—none other than Jimmy Stewart.

Harvey S. Firestone, showing President Harding around the camp at Hagerstown, Maryland. The July 23, 1921 visit included a lunch of lamb chops, ham, corn, potatoes, biscuits, watermelon and coffee – after which the President took a nap.
(Cleveland Public Library Photo Archives)

Appropriately, Ford, 53 years old in 1916, kept in constant motion and enjoyed outdoor activity. He took brisk walks, chopped wood for the campfires, and liked studying or repairing anything mechanical. Once he stopped the travelers to help a salesman fix his broken-down car. When the salesman insisted on paying for Ford's help, Ford refused, saying he was already a rich man. The man replied, skeptically, "If you're rich, why are you driving a Ford?"

The four celebrity tourists and their entourage were an imposing group. Along the road, the campers astounded individuals unaware of their trip.

Once at the gasoline pump of a Firestone dealer in the rural South, the attendant asked the famous travelers, "Who might you all be?"

"My name is Harvey S. Firestone."

The mountaineer sniffed and asked again, "Who's that man, over there?"

"That is Henry Ford."

"Humph—and the other one?"

"Thomas A. Edison."

"Huh—I suppose you'll be tellin' me in a minute that man in the front seat, with the white beard, is Santa Claus!"

He was, of course, Burroughs.

In 1929 Thomas Edison celebrated his 82nd birthday at a party in Florida attended by Herbert Hoover, Ford and Firestone. A few days later, Hoover would be sworn in as President of the United States.
(Martin Luther King Library, Washington D.C.)

Shying away from the many accomplishments that made their names household words, Henry Ford is content to call his famous friends, Thomas Edison and Harvey S. Firestone, simply "good campers."
(Bridgestone/Firestone Collection)

Four of the most renowned Americans of their day, and, perhaps, the world's most famed and photographed campers – Firestone, Ford, Edison, and Burroughs – pause for a news service photo.
(Bridgestone/Firestone Collection)

Good Campers in the End

Around campfires from the Catskills to the southern Appalachians, the four famous travelers enjoyed the outdoors and each other's company. Most of all, they enjoyed sharing ideas for the new century and its vast possibilities. Their conversations under the stars were wide-ranging.

According to Alfred Lief, Ford generally talked about mechanical things. Though all the campers were interested in the possibilities of hydroelectricity, Ford, in particular, was fascinated by the concept that flowing water could be used to generate power for the betterment of mankind. He often spoke of making the life of women easier with new electrical appliances.

Edison described complex theories of chemistry while Burroughs considered the birds, wildflowers, and his admiration for the ingenious use of natural resources by industry. As well as an environmentalist, Burroughs was an early advocate of businesses accepting social responsibility.

Firestone, it's said, tended to expound on his theories of business. He was particularly interested in the changing nature of the American workplace and the move from farm

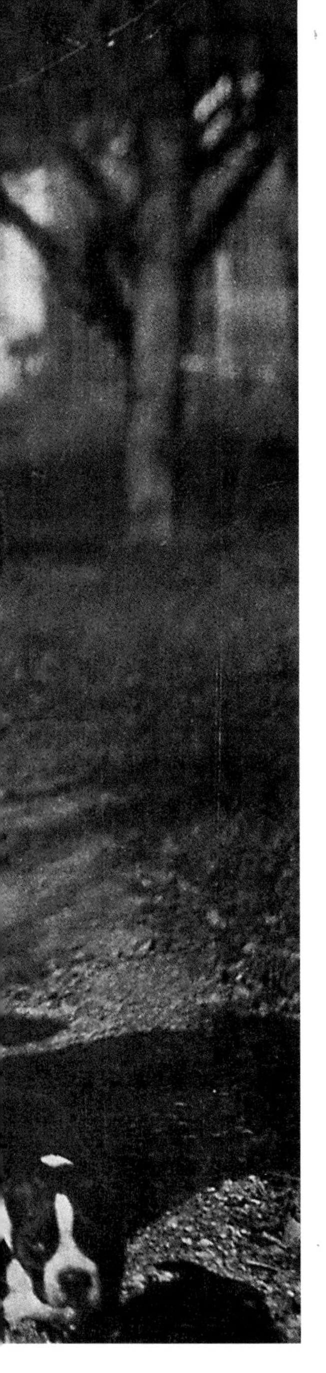

On March 9, 1931, Firestone visits with Edison for the last time at the Great Inventor's Fort Myers estate. In October of that same year, Edison died. Firestone paused in New York City on the night of his friend's passing to watch as the lights were turned out in tribute to the man who illuminated most of the world with his inventions.
(Russ Vitale Photography)

Firestone and Ford shared rural roots as well as a common desire to improve life on the farm. Here, Firestone sits atop a steel-wheeled tractor whose hard ride he would ease with a cushion of rubber.
(Bridgestone/Firestone Collection)

The founder's five sons – Roger, Russell, Harvey, Jr., Leonard, and Raymond – gather for the dedication of the Akron Memorial to Harvey S. Firestone, Sr.

(American Highway Users Alliance Archives)

to factory. Once near Martinsville, Virginia, Firestone visited a fabric mill operated by Marshall Field & Company of Chicago. The workers were men who had been brought down from the mountains, lean and undernourished, then given good homes and reasonable wages. Firestone was impressed with the industrial and social experiment at work here.

The success of the trips had a lot to do with ending them. Ford pronounced them good fun, "except that they began to attract too much attention." Firestone agreed. "We became a kind of traveling circus."

Finally, the death of John Burroughs in 1921 took something away from the trips. There would be no trip in 1922. And 1924 would be the last time Firestone, Ford and Edison would travel together.

When Harvey S. Firestone died in 1938, seven years after Edison, editorial writers wrote about his relationships with the century's greatest minds. It was as if the four campers epitomized the genius and determination of the new century they had helped launch.

Hearst newspapers reported, "Mr. Firestone was one of an intimate group, including Thomas A. Edison and Henry Ford, whose work was largely responsible for the growth of the immense industrial era at the turn of the century."

The *New York Journal & American* proclaimed, "The success of men like Firestone, Edison and Ford is not to be measured by their wealth and fame. They put together the invisible elements of brains and genius and the unused resources of a growing country, and created useful products...They are the creators of more than industry and wealth. They create jobs. They create homes. They lay the foundations of health and happiness and education for millions who profit by their genius and ambition."

Henry Ford, in the highest compliment he could muster, simply called his old friend Harvey S. Firestone a "good camper." He was also reminded of their very first meeting and the first tires that Firestone had sold him more than 40 years before.

"They are still on the car and still serviceable."

If nothing else, they had served to introduce Firestone to the world.

On the day of his funeral, all the Firestone plants and offices throughout the world closed. The list of Firestone locations was a testimony to what this remarkable man created. Tire plants in Los Angeles and Memphis were closed. So, too, were the cotton mills of New Bedford, Massachusetts, and Gastonia, North Carolina. All company-owned retail stores also shut their doors for the day. Operations fell silent in England, Argentina, South Africa, Switzerland, Spain, Singapore and Liberia.

He left the company in the hands of his family. His five sons—Harvey, Jr., Raymond, Leonard, Roger, and Russell—continued the journey their father had begun, through the 20th century.

"MERIT WILL WIN OUT..." THOUGHTS FROM THE FOUNDER

Though not known as an orator, Harvey S. Firestone was a great thinker who was given many occasions to speak his mind. Here are a few words that help reveal the voice of Firestone and the character of the man.

Firestone making a tire

(Bridgestone/Firestone Collection)

MERIT "Among many there is a belief that someone else gets the credit for his or her accomplishment. That is false. The one who puts forth the best effort will come out on top. Merit will win out."

HARD WORK "You don't get anything unless you work for it and there was never greater opportunity to succeed than there is today."

"You cannot get around difficulties. You have to overcome them."

SERVICE "Every useful occupation gives ample opportunity for service. The happiest men in the world are those who are making their jobs mean more than an endless routine of work and wages. The whole structure of business is based upon making useful things for others—this is service."

LEADERSHIP "It has been my experience that every department of the business rises or sinks to the level of the man at the head. Therefore, it devolves upon the company to pick men of good character as its executives."

"Success is the sum of detail."

"The weak man is the one who refuses to do any real thinking, or to make any sacrifice and he will not take on responsibility for himself or others. He is usually a pessimist, for it takes thought and imagination to be an optimist."

FARM LIFE "To me the American farm represents the spirit and fundamentals that have made America so great as a nation..."

Firestone
PLASTIC ELECTRICAL TAPE
Firestone
TUBE REPAIR KIT
Firestone
SYNTHETIC RUBBER & LATEX CO.
SECT U-U
SECT V
Firestone
EXTRA VALUE MERCHANDISE
SPRING AND SUMMER
1951
Home & Auto Supply

CHAPTER 3

RUNAWAY INVENTION

3

From tire treads to sexy threads and women's lingerie, Firestone never tires of innovation

The most memorable journeys are always filled with discoveries. And Firestone's incredible ride through the 20th century is no exception.

Discovery is at the heart of the Firestone story. As the character of the 20th century was defined by its major inventions—the automobile, the airplane, the telephone, the transistor, the rocket, and the computer—so was the character of Firestone.

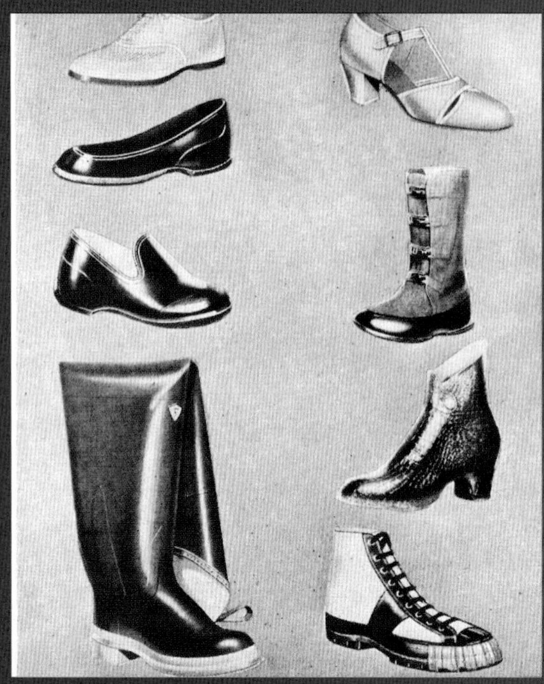

Traveling by car or by foot, Firestone had just the thing to fit your needs as shown here in a brochure distributed at the 1933 Chicago World's Fair.
(Bridgestone/Firestone Collection)

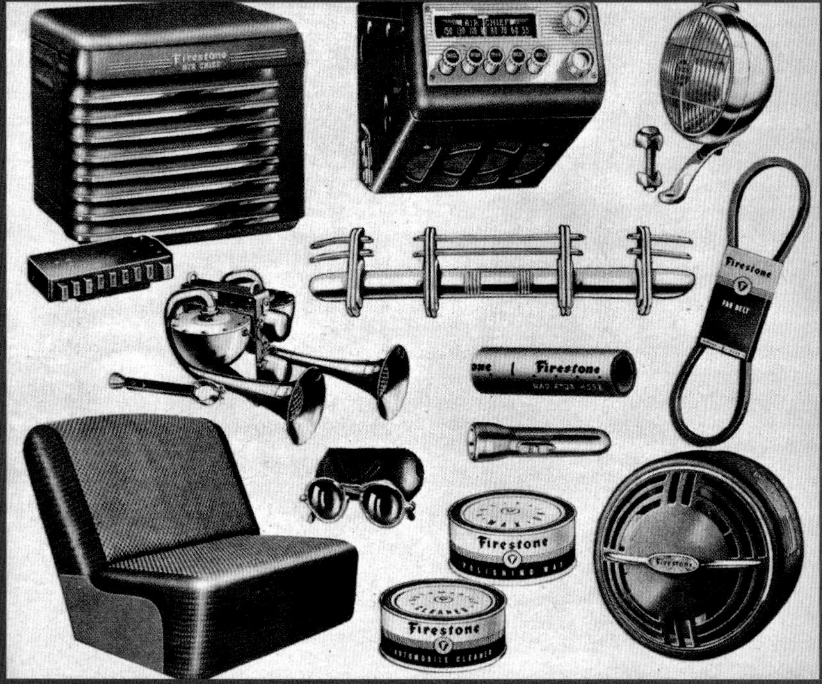

From car seats to sunglasses, a Firestone promotional piece for the 1939-1940 New York World's Fair highlights the company's versatility.
(Bridgestone/Firestone Collection)

"Let me take you for a moment on a flight of fancy into the World of Tomorrow. In the model postwar home, you may find rubber flooring, upholstery, mattresses, table tops, wall coverings, drapes, hose, weather stripping, insulation and toys. Milady's undergarments, evening gowns, handbags, footwear, stockings and hats may be made entirely or partly with rubber. The same is true of men's socks, underwear, shoes, pajamas, suspenders, garters and many other items."

– Harvey S. Firestone, Jr., to The Economic Club of Detroit following World War II

Beginning at the century's turn with tire manufacturing, Firestone quickly moved into other avenues—both automotive and beyond—to create an honored American name. Along the way, Firestone's inventive firsts served the globe. In times of need, Firestone provided jobs, defended freedom, loved the earth, explored the far-flung recesses of space, and drove us to our desired destinations with safety, comfort, and economy.

Although its many spinoff products have moved the company down many paths, Firestone is still a name known primarily for its tire and rubber technology. From its early solid rubber buggy tires to modern Firestone Indy racing tires, the company's history of innovation continues to revolve around tire technology.

Firestone demonstrates its wear – fashionwear, not tire wear – in this New York World's Fair display of Controlastic – "new multi-ply elastic yarn for foundation garments, bathing suits and other apparel where elasticity and figure control are of paramount importance." (Bridgestone/Firestone Collection)

The Tire's Turning Point

When Firestone was founded in 1900, the company's first challenge was to innovate within the circle of tires and rims. It proved an area of incredible opportunity. Firestone began by improving the way rubber horse-drawn carriage tires were secured to the wheels. Its "sidewire" device turned first-year sales of $110,000.

Next came the challenge of equipping horseless carriages with tires that accommodated the rough roads and allowed for the vehicle's increasing weight, speed, and power. The new softer, air-filled pneumatic tire was the perfect medium for the motorcar. Harvey S. Firestone's fellow stockholders saw little opportunity in a pneumatic tire market controlled by a monopoly. Firestone overcame this challenge by *innovating* rather than accepting the current *pneumatic* tire technology. Again he turned to the way the tire was attached to the rim.

Then as now, most people's only interaction with tires came when it was time to change them. And the "clincher" type pneumatic tire made this relationship difficult, at best. People

The patent that propelled The Firestone Tire & Rubber Company into business a century ago was for a "mechanically fastened" sidewire tire that proved far easier to change than the "clincher" whose removal required a crowbar and back-breaking effort.

(University of Akron Archives – Firestone Collection)

tolerated the clincher, but nobody liked it. Firestone saw the possibilities and responded to the market with innovation.

In 1904, Firestone developed the straight-sided pneumatic tire that could be easily changed in a matter of minutes with a wrench. The pneumatic's straight sides also allowed for more air capacity, delivered more cushion to the passenger and more tire to the road. Firestone shared this pneumatic tire with Ford, and 2,000 sets of these tires are what began the longtime relationship between the two men's companies. It was the largest tire order ever placed up to that time and the turning point for Firestone.

In 1907, the company moved ahead with its third major innovation—the demountable rim for pneumatic automobile tires—another advancement in consumer convenience. Firestone's new rim could be taken off the wheels and replaced with another rim already mounted with an inflated tire. Competitors argued publicly that the average motorist didn't need a demountable rim and that this quick-change device was better suited for auto racing. Firestone let the market decide for itself, sending company representatives on the road for public demonstrations of the ease and convenience of the demountable rim. Within a year, Firestone's latest innovation was so successful that a demountable rim for truck tires was also introduced.

In 1908, truck transportation was more of a novelty than commonplace. Because of their weight and the road conditions, trucks rode on heavy solid rubber tires that were extremely hard to change. With no truck service stations to do the job, few businessmen risked trucking their goods for fear of breakdowns. The introduction of the demountable rim for solid truck tires led to the increased use of trucks.

Firestone continued to build its reputation on innovations that treated product challenges as marketing opportunities. One such popular improvement was the Firestone Non-Skid treaded tire.

Early tires' smooth tread made controlling the vehicle extremely difficult, especially when stopping a car at ever-higher speeds. To overcome the tire's lack of traction and a car's tendency to skid, tire makers added metal rivets and rippled leather to their rubber recipe or molded round rubber buttons to the tire's

In its early advertising, Firestone focused on quality and consumer-pleasing innovations, characteristics that drove the company's immediate success.
(Bridgestone/Firestone Collection)

In honor of his company's 30th anniversary in 1930, Harvey S. Firestone celebrates the changing times as well as changing tire technology, as he poses with an early pneumatic tire and one of the giant tires used for heavy equipment.
(University of Akron Archives – Firestone Collection)

More than 60 years of Firestone advances in fabric and synthetic cords improved tire life and performance and led to important product breakthroughs including the tubeless tire.
(Bridgestone/Firestone Collection)

surface. Finally, Harvey S. Firestone introduced a revolutionary principle incorporated into all anti-skid tires since 1908—the first angular tread. He had his engineers make the words "Firestone Non-Skid" part of the tread, a brilliant concept that served as both a technological breakthrough and a marketing bonanza.

Gum-Dipping and Cool Cords

Much of the credit for The Firestone Tire & Rubber Company's solid technological base goes to Chemist John W. Thomas. Thomas was hired as the company's first research director in 1908. His work was so respected that Thomas eventually led the corporation as its president and later as chairman of the board. One key development under Thomas's leadership was the process of gum-dipping cord fabric.

In 1915, the search for increased tire strength led to the first experiments using cord fabric for tire plies instead of the square-woven cloth previously used. More flexible and resilient, cords proved a great improvement, doubling a tire's life. However, internal friction created intense heat buildup which caused the tire to separate. This could be a major disaster.

The "Firestone Boys" proudly show off the new gum-dipped balloon tires that first appeared at the Indianapolis 500 in 1925, and continued Firestone's winning streak. (Bridgestone/Firestone Collection)

In 1920, Firestone's engineers finally perfected a method of "gum-dipping" cords to completely impregnate them with rubber, insulating them against heat build-up and ply separation and increasing the life of the tire.

One good turn deserved another. Along with dramatically improving tire wear and resiliency, gum-dipping allowed for another major Firestone first—the balloon, or low-pressure, tire. Softer balloon tires made the hard tire casing a thing of the past. They provided more cushion and lessened the shock to the car and the passenger. They also greatly reduced the danger of high-pressure blowouts. Firestone engineers produced the first practical set of low-pressure tires in October 1922. Factory production began the next April. Within a few years, Firestone's balloon tire was the standard tire for the world.

Progress in cord technology made possible another Firestone advance—the tubeless tire. Creating the tubeless tire required stronger cords using man-made fabrics. The cost of using cotton cords would have been prohibitive. Not only was cotton more expensive, but 15 to 20 percent more cotton than synthetic fibers was required for a fabric of equal strength. Rayon was used initially but it quickly opened the door to nylon, polyester, fiberglass, and steel. In 1951, after extensive research, synthetic cords were advanced to the point that the company introduced its tubeless tire.

Fire
Reaches a
to give Most M
Canadian Fireston
Factory
Hamilton
Footwear Factory
Boston
Cotton Mills
Fall River
AKRON
New Bedford
Cotton Mills
New York
Long Island
UNITED
Main Tire & Rim
Factories
at Akron - Ohio
STATES
Los Angeles
Firestone Factory
From
Singapore
Cotton
Plantations
ATLANTIC
OCEAN
GULF of MEXICO
Legend
Factories
Plantation buying
Offices
MEXICO
CUBA
JAMAICA
HAITI
PACIFIC
OCEAN
CARIBBEAN SEA
Ernest Clegg

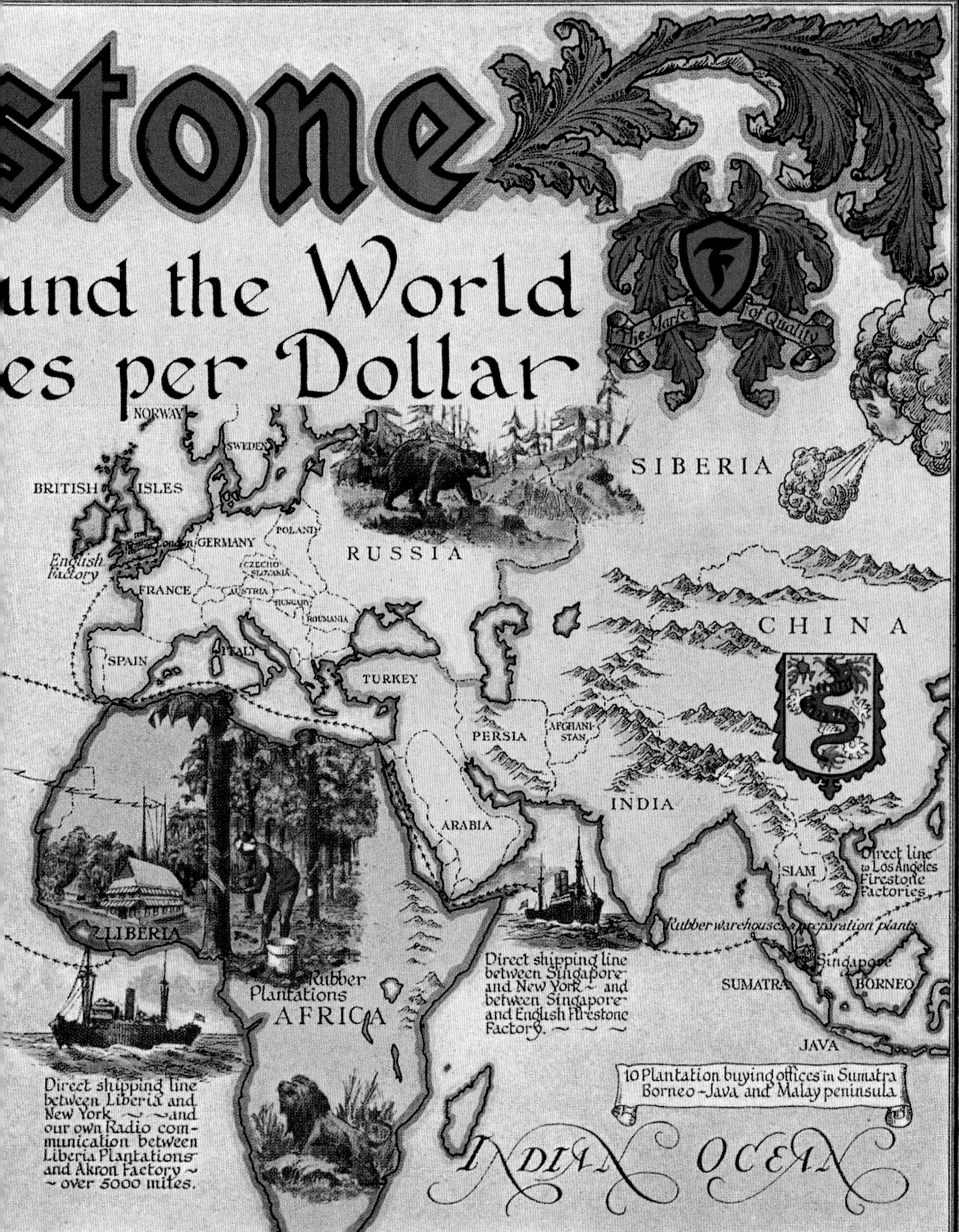
stone
und the World
es per Dollar
The Mark of Quality
NORWAY
SWEDEN
BRITISH ISLES
London
GERMANY
POLAND
RUSSIA
SIBERIA
English Factory
CZECHO SLAVANIA
FRANCE
AUSTRIA
HUNGARY
ROUMANIA
CHINA
SPAIN
ITALY
TURKEY
PERSIA
AFGHANISTAN
INDIA
ARABIA
SIAM
Direct line to Los Angeles Firestone Factories
Rubber warehouses & preparation plants
LIBERIA
Rubber Plantations
AFRICA
Direct shipping line between Singapore and New York ~ and between Singapore and English Firestone Factory. ~ ~ ~
Singapore
SUMATRA
BORNEO
JAVA
10 Plantation buying offices in Sumatra Borneo - Java and Malay peninsula
Direct shipping line between Liberia and New York ~ ~ and our own Radio communication between Liberia Plantations and Akron Factory ~ ~ over 5000 miles.
INDIAN OCEAN

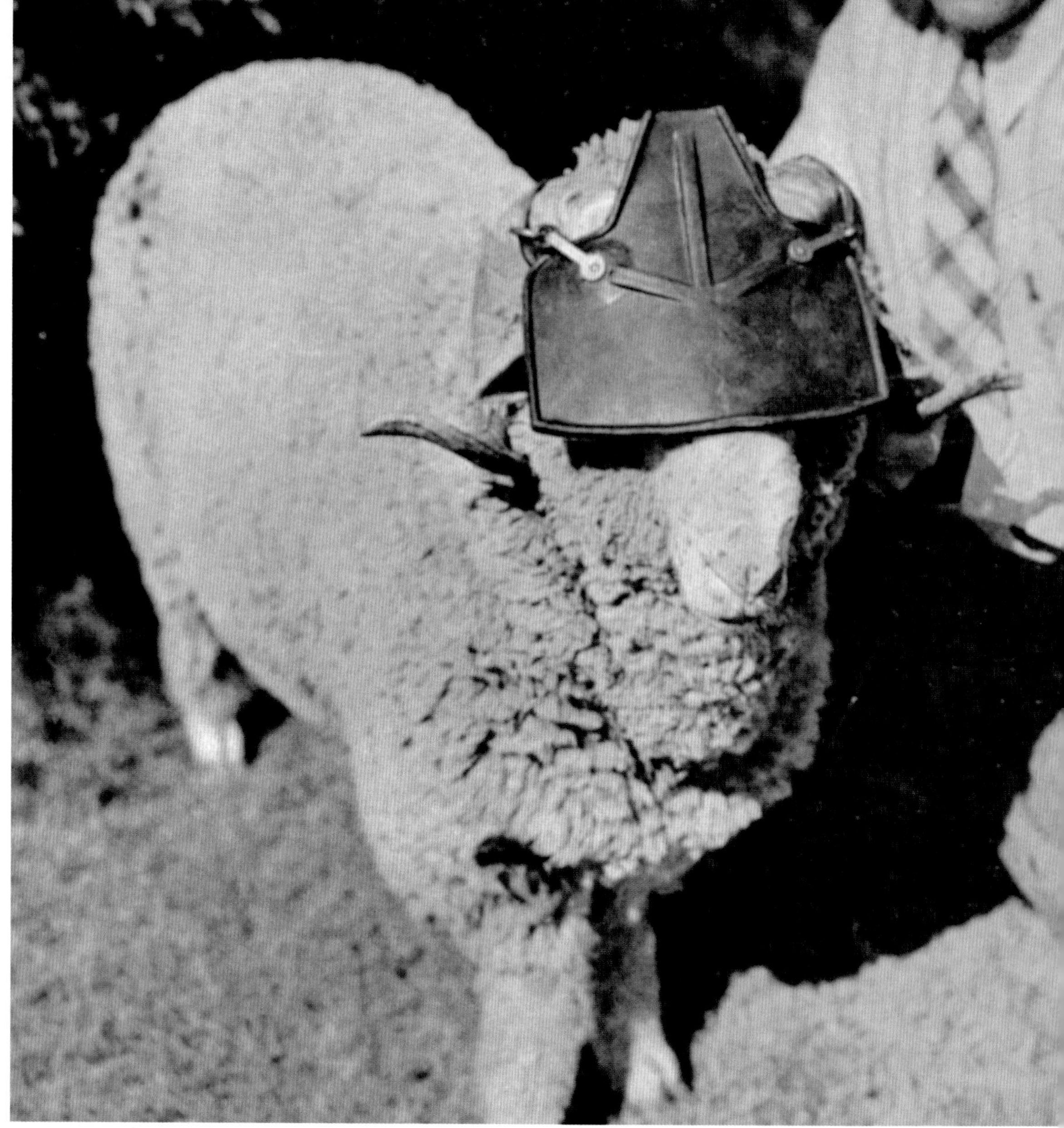

Of all the creative uses for rubber pioneered by Firestone, one of the most unusual may have been rubber masks for rams. Featured in a 1940 issue of *National Geographic*, the rubber mask allowed a ram to see its food but not its enemies when lowering its head into the fighting position.
(National Geographic, February 1940)

(Previous page) By 1928, Firestone is more than household name. It is a worldwide icon. This ad from that period shows the lengths to which Firestone goes – literally traveling the globe – to provide customers with a product that promises the "most miles per dollar."
(Bridgestone/Firestone Collection)

Sometimes Bigger Really Is Better

In 1935, Firestone discovered the way to create a bigger market for its tires was to craft a bigger tire.

Firestone's leadership in huge off-road tires used by large earthmoving and mining machines grew from Harvey S. Firestone's life-long interest in the farm. Because of his desire to ease the burden on farmers and put the "farm on rubber," his company enjoyed extensive experience in crafting oversized and special purpose tires.

"Anyone can build a tractor tire with deep tread," a company spokesman explained. "But in order to really help a farm, a tractor tire tread must be designed so as not to become clogged with mud when plowing. It must have superior traction qualities under many kinds of conditions, and must withstand wear when driven on surfaced roads."

The same performance characteristics necessary for farm tractor tires proved important to earthmovers. Both must withstand incredible abuse from sharp rocks, provide traction and be easy to retread.

At the request of contractors, the company crafted its first set of giant tires in 1935, using the expertise gained developing tractor tires. The tires were put to use on an earthmoving machine at a dam project in Cadiz, Ohio.

As with the early auto industry, Firestone's move into larger, specialized tires helped move the heavy equipment industry forward.

As the 21st century begins, Bridgestone/Firestone is a leader in the earthmoving tire industry in both bias and radial. Today, the

A Real Big Wheel

Let's face it—Tires aren't very photogenic...even with snappy hubcaps, white sidewalls, or high-tech tread. Presenting tires in the best possible light has long been a challenge for Firestone advertising and public relations.

So, the big, oversized tire, just the right size for all kinds of humans—starlets, actors, clowns, and athletes—to appear with was a real boon to tire promotion. When Jack Dempsey, the former heavyweight champion of the world, was promoting a car racing movie called *The Big Wheel,* he came to the factory in Akron to pose inside the biggest tire in the plant. Harvey S. Firestone himself, less than average height, loved to pose next to his big truck and tractor tires.

In honor of the founder's 50th birthday, Firestone held an indoor exposition in Akron. However, the Firestone 30.00 x 40 Heavy Duty Ground Grip "Earth Moving" 8.5-foot-tall monster tire was too large to display inside of the exposition. So it was placed on the flower-decked terrace, adjacent to the exposition hall. Suddenly the hole, and not the donut, was the story. Everyone from Prince Paul, a famous Ringling Brothers and Barnum and Bailey Circus clown, to major league baseball players, posed inside the tire. Big tires made for great photographs. It's a tradition that continues today.

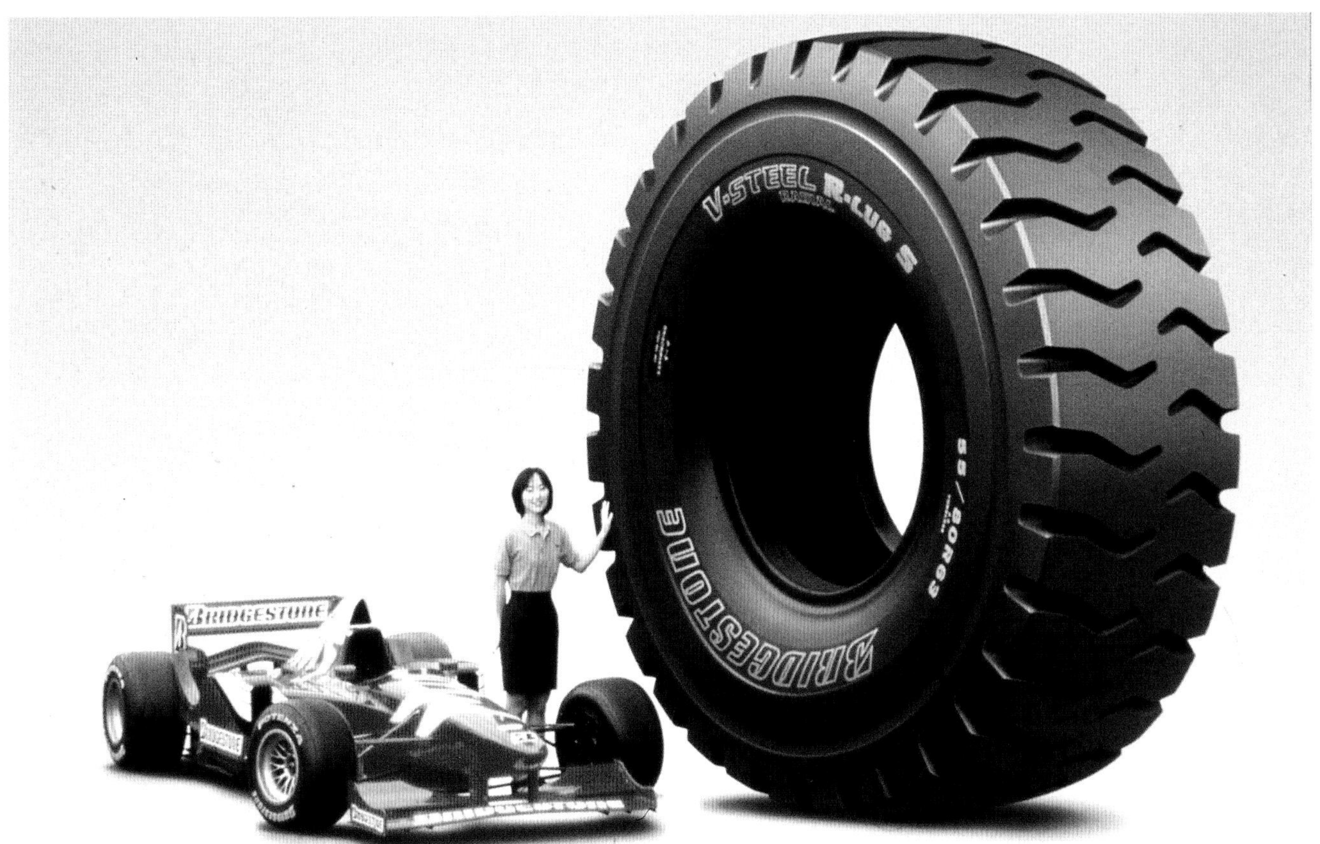

Bridgestone Corporation in Japan and Bridgestone/Firestone build on the tradition of providing performance tires for jobs of all sizes, from its high-performance Formula 1 racing tires to the world's largest radial tire at 12-feet-10-inches tall and weighing 4.7 tons. (Bridgestone/Firestone Collection)

Caterpillar hauling truck used in mines all over the world, equipped with Firestone tires.
(Bridgestone/Firestone Collection)

company crafts tires for the construction and mining industries, ranging in size from 22 inches to nearly 13 feet tall and weighing up to an amazing 12,000 pounds.

What began as the founder's romantic attachment to the farm has plowed new ground for growth and reaped major financial rewards for the company.

Rubber Goes to War

Of all the market challenges Firestone faced and overcame in its first 40 years of innovation, none ranked higher in the life of the company or country than World War II. It was the first major battle Firestone waged without the leadership of its founder, Harvey S. Firestone. The war effort's unparalleled demand for rubber and manufacturing muscle stretched the company's capabilities to the limit but also better prepared it to meet the post-war boom.

First Firestone had to help ease the country's critical need for rubber.

In 1942, with World War II in full swing, concern over the Allied Forces' rubber supply prompted President Franklin D. Roosevelt to call on one of his most trusted advisors, Bernard Baruch, to determine the effect of rubber shortages on the outcome of the war. No rubber was produced in North America and the war was cutting off important rubber sources.

Baruch, one of the era's premier industrialists, organized a blue-ribbon presidential commission whose distinguished members included James B. Conant, president of Harvard University, and Kart T. Compton, president of the Massachusetts Institute of Technology. The panel concluded that the potential shortage of natural rubber was the "greatest threat" to the United States war efforts.

The commission demanded an immediate and dramatic increase in research, development, and production of synthetic rubber. Delay, it said, meant "the successful operation of our mechanized army would be jeopardized."

As if the message were not clear enough, it added this dire warning: "We find the existing situation to be so dangerous that unless corrective measures are taken immediately, this country will face both military and a civilian collapse."

The desperate need for rubber was obvious. Military forces rolled into battle aboard a mountain of rubber. Each battleship required 75 tons. Each armored tank used a ton. Each B-17 Flying Fortress required a half-ton. The combat-ready, super-tough tires the armed forces used in great numbers took six times more rubber and five times more fabric than the most popular size of passenger car tire.

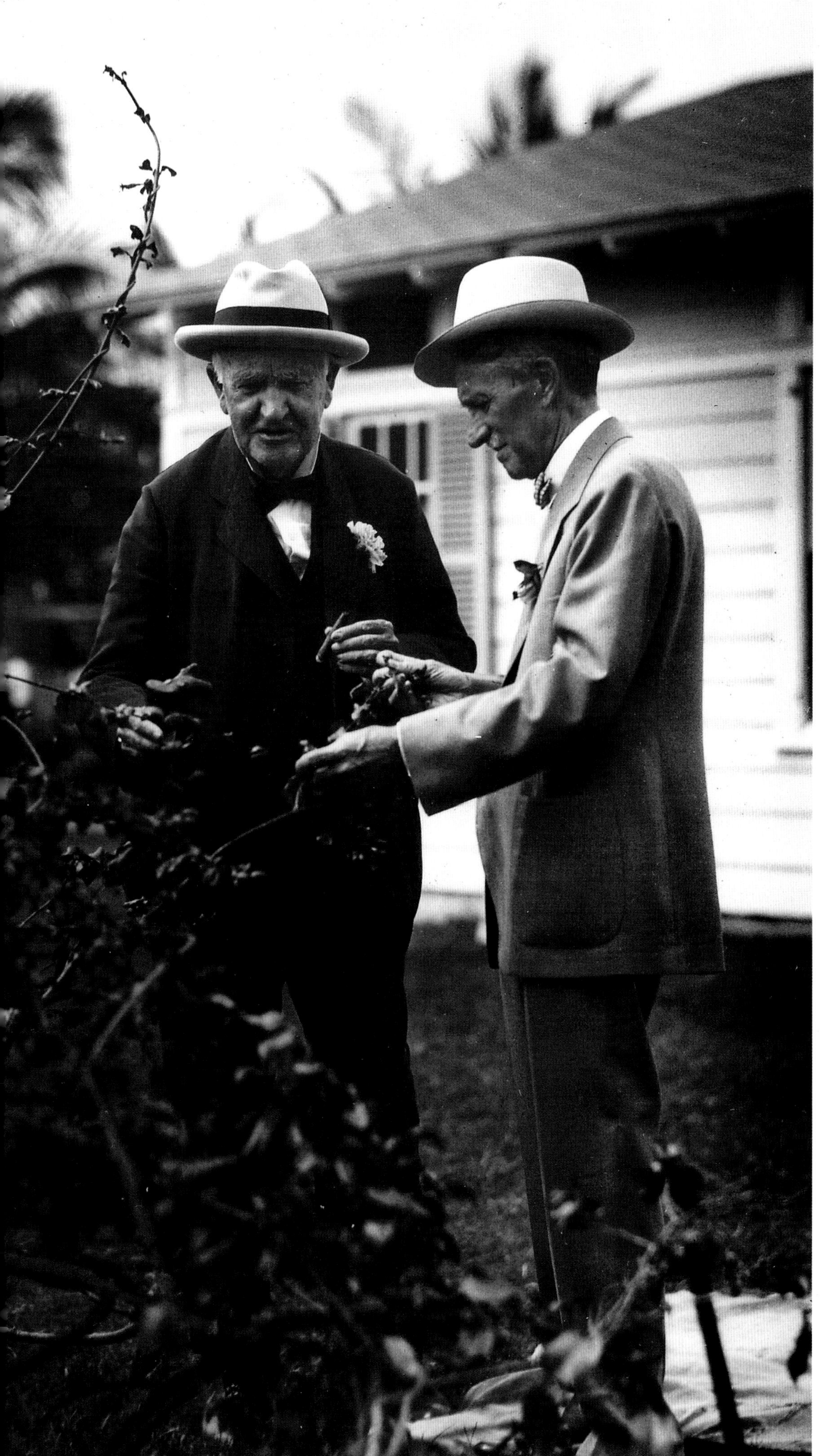

As early as 1925, Thomas Edison was looking for an alternative source of rubber and believed the answer lay in a common plant that could be harvested like wheat. Here, Edison and Firestone examine one of the inventor's experiments to coax latex from a native plant source – goldenrod.
(Russ Vitale Photography)

President Roosevelt concurred with the Baruch Commission and issued an order that set in motion a massive undertaking that combined the capacity and expertise of The Firestone Tire & Rubber Company and its competitors. According to the *Akron Beacon Journal,* this launched an effort that "outranked every World War II priority."

Working with a special emergency antitrust exemption, the major rubber companies formed a consortium charged with increasing rubber production. All were required to share their technological expertise in producing synthetic rubber. Working together, the American rubber industry soon discovered the recipe for a suitable synthetic.

Synthetic rubber production, only 8,000 tons in 1941, quickly rose to 230,000 tons in 1943, and bounced even higher, to 750,000 tons, in 1944. As the war ended in 1945, the nation was producing one million tons—the level targeted by the Baruch Commission to achieve victory.

A government report, *Tires at War,* issued on April 16, 1945, said, "The synthetic rubber program was the greatest challenge ever hurled at the American free enterprise system. Accepting the challenge, the rubber industry, in cooperation with the government and other industries, mobilized its army of chemists, engineers, and production experts and did the job.

"Sky-scraper synthetic rubber plants have mushroomed up at strategic points all over the country. The one thing that America lacked to win the war, America took out of the test tube and built in 18 months into a billion dollar industry."

Harvey S. Firestone, Jr., (left) shows Harvey D. Gibson, the New York World's Fair Chairman of the Board, a piece of synthetic rubber sheet used to craft tires at the fair's working tire factory in the Firestone Pavilion. The first public demonstration of synthetic rubber tire manufacturing took place at the World's Fair in 1940 on the day the company turned 40.

(University of Akron Archives – Firestone Collection)

"Americans ~~should~~ do produce their own rubber"

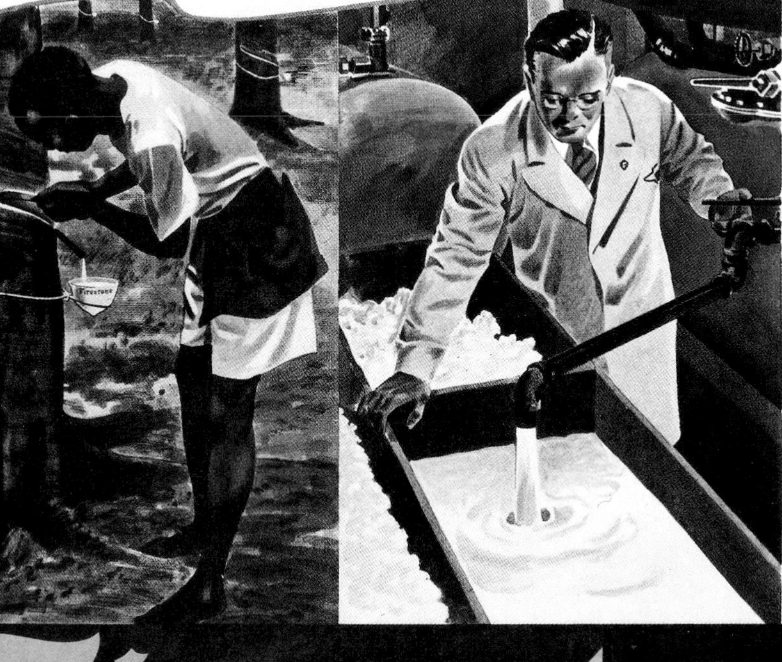

MORE than twenty years ago, Harvey S. Firestone urged that this country make itself independent of all foreign-controlled sources of rubber. He took the leadership in this cause under the banner "Americans should produce their own rubber."

He advocated three ways by which this could be accomplished — first, by establishing rubber plantations under American control in friendly nations—second, by obtaining rubber from domestic plants—and third, by making rubber synthetically.

After a world-wide survey, he established the Firestone Rubber Plantations in Liberia, one of the few remaining sources from which the United States is still obtaining natural rubber. Working with Thomas A. Edison, they investigated many types of domestic plants as possible sources of rubber. In the Firestone Research Laboratories, he directed his scientists in the study and development of synthetic rubber and in 1940 Firestone began producing its own synthetic rubber, Butaprene, the same type which was later adopted by the Government. With this unsurpassed experience, the Firestone organization naturally took a position of leadership in attacking the rubber problems which confronted our country after Pearl Harbor.

Today, Americans *do* produce their own rubber, both natural and synthetic. They know how to grow it, they know how to make it and they know how to use it! And Harvey S. Firestone will be remembered forever as a true patriot who initiated and inspired this vitally important forward step in American economic freedom.

☆

For the best in music, listen to the "Voice of Firestone" with Richard Crooks and Gladys Swarthout and the Firestone Symphony Orchestra conducted by Howard Barlow every Monday evening over NBC network.

Copyright, 1944, The Firestone Tire & Rubber Co.

Firestone

PIONEER AND PACEMAKER

Firestone
BEST
IN RUBBER

For decades prior to World War II, Firestone foresaw the dangers of depending on foreign sources for rubber, and advertised its concern that "Americans should produce their own rubber." Ultimately, Firestone helped answer the issue it raised by producing its own synthetic rubber. (Bridgestone/Firestone Collection)

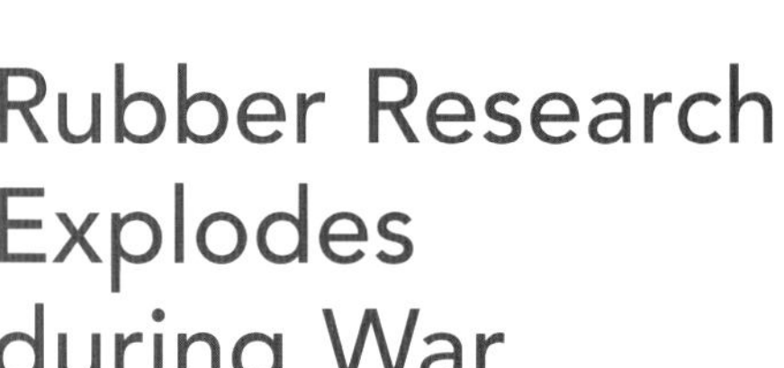

Rubber Research Explodes during War

World War II proved to be critical turning point in rubber and tire research. Before the conflict, most tires were made from natural rubber, a yellowish elastic material obtained from the milky sap of various tropical plants. The plants grew in Southeast Asia, and areas of the world subject to political unrest or susceptible to capture and blockades by enemies of the United States. The result was an unreliable supply of rubber. For decades before the war, Firestone had advertised its concern that "Americans should produce their own rubber."

Luther Burbank and Thomas Edison had combed the plant life of America seeking rubber-producing growths. Edison's explorations had been encouraged by his old camping companions Firestone and Ford as early as 1925.

The heightened wartime research in the 1940s found a solution in a synthetic made chiefly from styrene and butadiene. The two were derived from petroleum and coal-fed stocks. Within a short time, tires were crafted almost exclusively from synthetic rubber. By 1947, Firestone's output of synthetic rubber exceeded its imports from its Harbel plantation in Liberia.

The wartime boom in rubber production led to a postwar surge in innovative ways to use the readily available rubber. Consumers were hit with a postwar barrage of rubber products—from brake linings to lingerie.

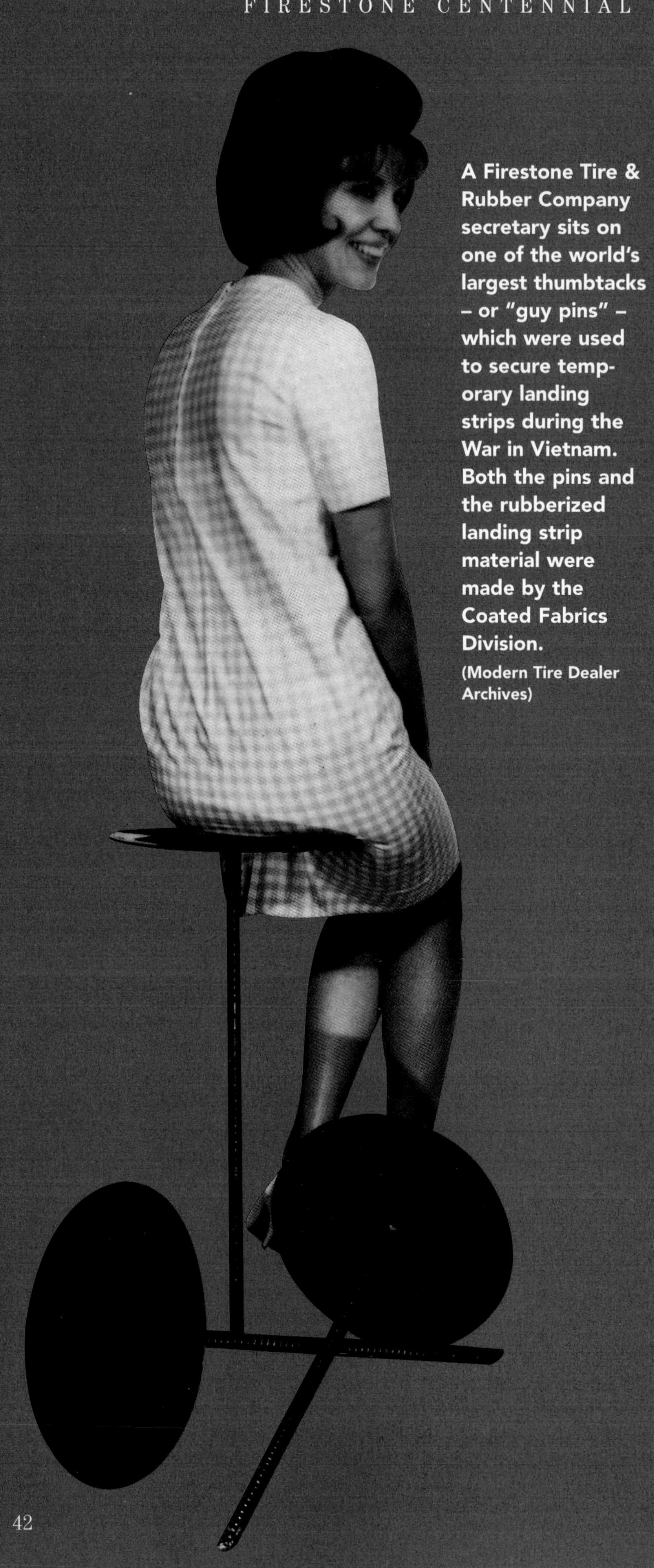

A Firestone Tire & Rubber Company secretary sits on one of the world's largest thumbtacks – or "guy pins" – which were used to secure temporary landing strips during the War in Vietnam. Both the pins and the rubberized landing strip material were made by the Coated Fabrics Division.
(Modern Tire Dealer Archives)

RUBBER-COATING THE WORLD

Instead of sugar-coating things, Firestone's ability to rubber-coat fabrics has made life just a little bit easier.

Firestone discovered it could craft everything from blankets to fuel cells with rubberized fabric. For the military, it produced life rafts, pontoon bridges, and water and fuel storage tanks. In 1964, the company received a large contract for producing airfield fuel dispensing systems. Coated fabric tanks could be installed on the beaches or shorelines and then filled with a line from an off-shore tanker whose tanks could hold as much as 10,000 gallons of fuel.

Another wartime use for coated fabric was in the construction of instantaneous landing strips during the Vietnam Era. Landing strips were dusty or muddy if left uncovered. Firestone developed a coated fabric carpet that was rolled out over a newly graded airfield and held in place by giant tacks. When planes and helicopters made their approach to the rubberized airfield, they weren't blinded by the dust and flying debris.

All Things Rubber

It was Harvey S. Firestone, Jr., who claimed, "...you can do almost anything with rubber but eat it." The company founded by his father in 1900 proved his conclusion correct. Throughout the course of the company's 100-year existence, thousands of products other than tires have spun off from Firestone research.

In the 1934 annual report to stockholders, the company noted that, "While Firestone for 34 years has been associated mainly with tires, yet your company manufactures not only tires, tubes, and rims for automobiles, trucks, buses, tractors, and farm implements, but also spark plugs, brake linings, auto supplies, motor supports, vibration dampeners, wringer rolls, footwear, and many other rubber specialities."

The car of the '30s was crafted with more than 100 rubber parts, providing added comfort, safety, and economy. Firestone branched out from these automotive needs to encompass other transportation vehicles as well as non-transportation products. Street cars and trackless trolleys were cushioned with 56 Firestone rubber parts. Streamline trains used the company's air brake hoses and other rubber parts. Washing machines were made more efficient with Firestone wringer rollers. Power plants, factories, and steamships reduced vibration and wear with Firestone rubber vibration dampeners.

Increasingly, other parts of the company devoted themselves to a diverse number of products including rubber thread for golf balls, cushions for gun butts and bumpers, plastic cases for radios and batteries, and elastic for lingerie and bathing suits. In all, by 1940, the company was making 500 different types of rubber products. This was only the beginning. In 1955, still in the war's wake, the company added more than 400 new mechanical and rubber goods to its product line.

Firestone's research on synthetic rubber in the 1930s led to what is now Firestone Polymers, a division that operates state-of-the-art research, development, and technical service laboratories and a pilot plant in Akron, Ohio, as well as manufacturing facilities in Lake Charles, Louisiana, and Orange, Texas.

Today Firestone's synthetic rubber is used in television and VCR cabinets, conveyer belts, medical equipment and supplies, food containers, flooring, toys, and adhesives for diapers. Even so, nearly 50 percent of the company's synthetic rubber is still used for tires.

Firestone's entry into the plastics business was a natural outgrowth of its work with rubber. Essentially rubber is a form of plastic and many of the basic manufacturing processes are the same. Development work in the 1930s led to the extrusion of a vinyl monofilament and a move into plastics.

With its work in plastics, the company built a synthetic fibers division. Although initially created to control costs and quality of tire building materials, the division expanded into fibers for other applications. From plastics, it was a logical detour into chemicals, a broad field that included adhesives, new synthetics, and metal processing.

The non-tire business was good for the company, bringing in profits disproportionate to its total sales. By 1975, tires and related products amounted to 81 percent of sales but only 68 percent of company profits.

Firestone Tests Its Metal

Firestone's interest in steel products came early in its history, again as a logical outgrowth of its tire business. The company's introduction of the first demountable rim in 1907 led to a rim manufacturing division in 1909 that became the nation's largest rim producer. Rims eventually led to automotive body stampings, then to cabinets and miscellaneous stamped parts.

In 1933, the company rolled out a line of stainless steel beer barrels, a move that worried the guardians of the corporate reputation. Beer still carried an unsavory connotation even in the era following the repeal of the Volstead Act and the end of Prohibition. The company's founder, a teetotaller, had favored Prohibition. For many years, Firestone talked of its work with "beverage" containers, avoiding the word "beer." As America again became a beer-consuming nation, the container market surged and Firestone's outpouring of steel containers quickly washed away the wooden beer barrel.

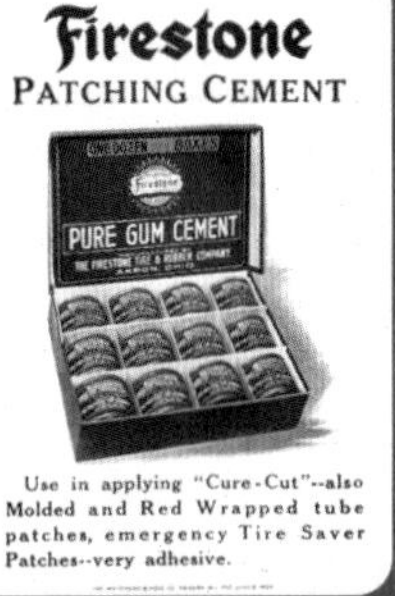

From tire tape to pure gum patching cement, celluloid trading cards show the diversity of tire care products offered by Firestone as early as 1905. (Bridgestone/Firestone Collection)

Exploring the "one-stop shop" concept during the 1930s, Firestone and Firestone Dealer stores carried a number of household goods from refrigerators to rakes.
(Bridgestone/Firestone Collection)

While building a better barrel, Firestone also built up its expertise in stainless steel and welding. This earned the company preferential treatment when steel products were needed for national defense. In fact, war, and preparation for war, led to many new opportunities. During World War II and the Korean conflict, Firestone became a leading supplier of helmet liners, molded with nylon fiber and impregnated with plastic for greater protection from shrapnel and bullets. In 1943, the company produced its two-millionth helmet liner and, that same year, proudly flew the Army-Navy "E" award for excellence in defense production at its Fall River plant in Massachusetts.

Following the Korean conflict, nickel was again available for civilian use and the company resumed manufacturing of stainless steel beverage containers. A quarter-barrel size was introduced. Now the company's container line added milk cans and soft drink dispenser machines to its mix, becoming the world's largest manufacturer of containers.

From containers came jet engine components and metal parts for television tubes. Other experiments led to a very lucrative product line as car manufacturers became interested in colored aluminum stamping for automobile grills and trim parts.

Firestone set up a major aluminum anodizing operation in Akron. The equipment turned out bright-dip grills and colored door trim parts for 1958 cars. An imaginative manufacturing process permitted the automated production of car parts in various colors and finishes. Anodized aluminum was etched, brushed, or buffed for a variety of textures, dulled for a matte finish, or chemically brightened to resemble chrome.

Industrial Products Spring Up

The late 1920s saw the beginning of another division, the Firestone Industrial Products Company. Firestone began making manufactured mechanical rubber goods in a back corner of Plant Number 1 in Akron after Ford Motor Company expressed an interest in rubber molded

During the early 1970s, the pandas at the National Zoo in Washington, D.C., destroyed toys at an alarming rate. Firestone Steel Products of Spartanburg, South Carolina, came to the rescue with stainless-steel barrels that proved to be panda-proof toys.
(Modern Tire Dealer Archives)

running boards. The line grew to include rubber engine mounts, hoses, crank shaft dampers, seat cushions, and many other items.

From a single plant in 1936, Firestone Industrial Products grew into a multinational manufacturing and distribution company. Its growth was accelerated with key product developments such as an innovative Firestone air spring system.

Firestone's air spring system was pioneered right after World War II and finally introduced in 1953 in a General Motors-built bus delivered to Greyhound. The system was an immediate success because it made the ride more comfortable for passengers while saving the vehicle from the destructive shaking produced by existing suspension and spring systems.

In fact, in the first year Firestone air springs were used, Greyhound estimated a $1 million savings in vehicle damage. Soon Firestone air springs were the standard for all bus companies. Trucks followed and certain applications saw immediate success.

An inflatable dam, manufactured by The Firestone Tire & Rubber Company, spans 150 feet across the Los Angeles River. The remarkable rubber dam, which is inflated by pumping water into it, can be collapsed in ten minutes.
(Bridgestone/Firestone Collection)

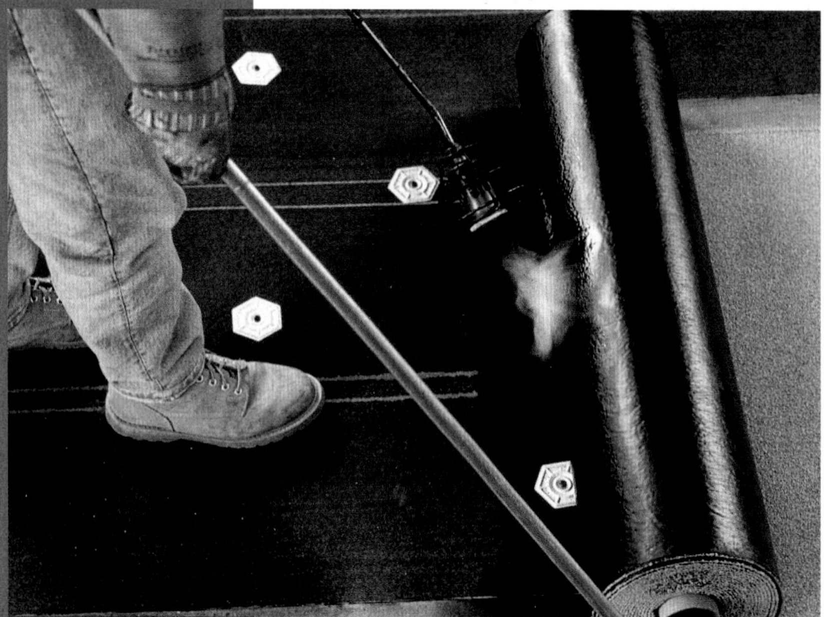

Torch application of a modified bitumen membrane.
(Roofing/Building Products)

Today, Firestone Industrial Products Company can boast designing and building more air springs for more applications than any other air spring company in the world. In fact, more than half of all trucks in the United States are equipped with Firestone Airide springs.

Firestone from Floor to Ceiling

During the '60s, Firestone innovations took an important turn which carried the company down profitable new business avenues. The rubber technology that put us on the open road also improved the life of structures we visit.

In 1960, Firestone unveiled a new weather-resistant expansion joint material, Flex-Time, which virtually eliminated cracking in seams of terrazzo tile and concrete flooring. The new rubber compound withstood the punishment of traffic, moisture, oil, and other deteriorating agents that separated the tile from cement.

In the late '70s, further work introduced a single-ply rubber roofing that became so successful that it was spun off into another division called the Firestone Building Products Company. Today this division is the leading player in the highly competitive commercial roofing industry. Millions of square feet of Firestone roofing systems have been installed on commercial facilities worldwide.

Textiles used in the reinforcement of its tires were once produced at the Loray Mill Firestone Textile Plant in Gastonia, North Carolina. Nearly a century old, the historically significant structure was donated by Bridgestone/Firestone, Inc. to Preservation North Carolina in 1998.
(Bridgestone/Firestone Collection)

Four of Harvey S. Firestone's sons gather around the globe to map the company's worldwide operations at the time of Firestone Tire & Rubber Company's 60th anniversary. Harvey S. Firestone, Jr., chairman and chief executive officer, points out a new plant in Orange, Texas, to brothers Leonard K. Firestone, president of the Firestone Tire & Rubber Company of California; Raymond C. Firestone, president of the parent company; and Roger S. Firestone, president of the Firestone Plastics Company of Pottstown, Pennsylvania. (American Highway Users Alliance Archives)

Another thread that ties Firestone's early history to Bridgestone/Firestone's business today is cotton. A key ingredient in tire reinforcement, Firestone sought to better manage fiber and textile production, much as it had alternative natural rubber sources, in order to ensure quality and value through a vertically integrated manufacturing company. In 1935, Firestone began producing tire reinforcement materials from cotton at the former Loray Mill in Gastonia, North Carolina. Built near the turn of the century in 1902 and expanded in 1921, the Loray Mill was one of North Carolina's most significant historic industrial properties and was finally donated by the company to Preservation North Carolina in 1998. Firestone

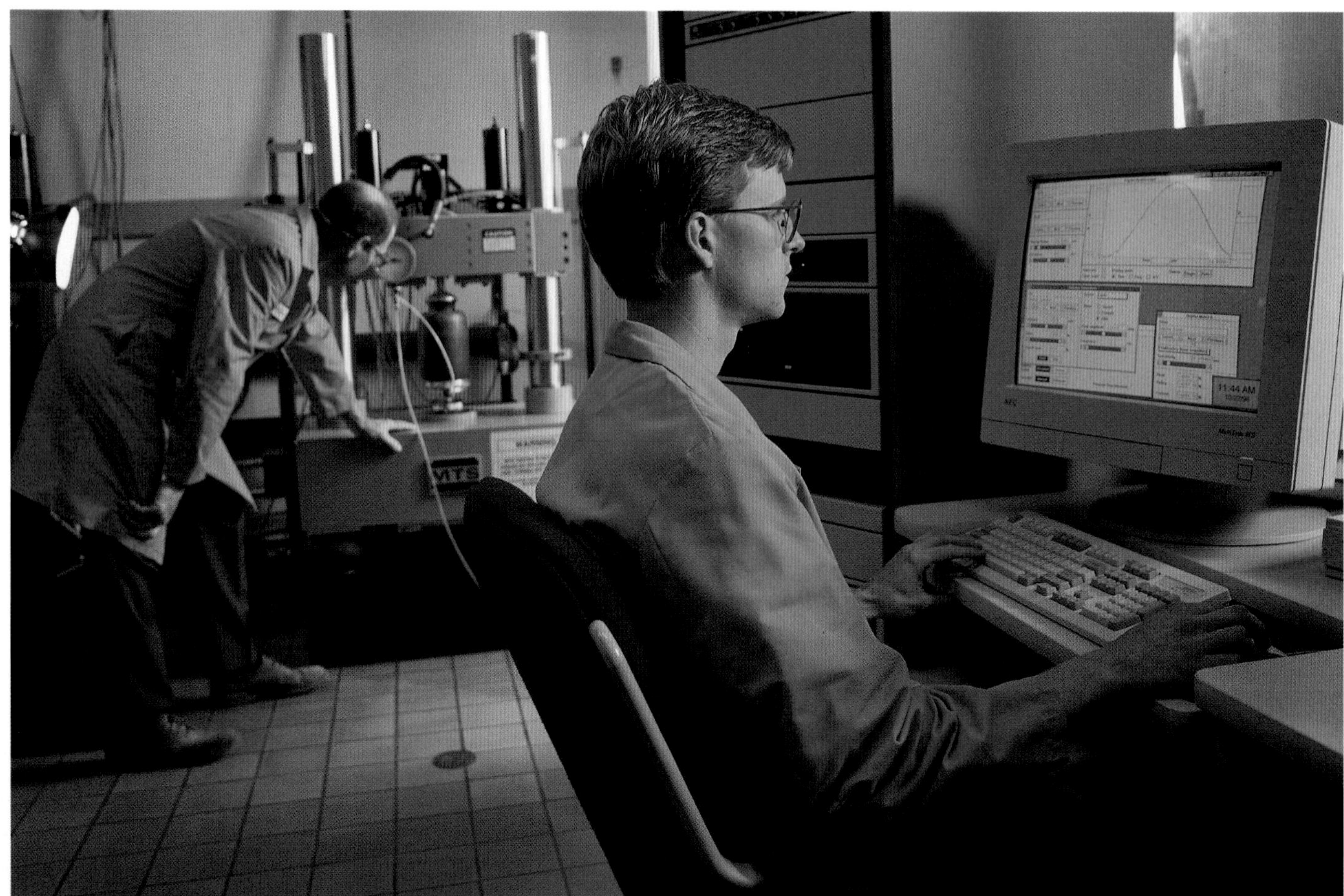

State-of-the-art-technology is used at Firestone's Akron Tech Center to test consumer tires for noise and vibration.
(Bridgestone/Firestone Collection)

moved out of the historic structure in 1993, when it began operations at a new facility a few miles away in Kings Mountain, North Carolina.

Today the Firestone Fibers and Textiles Company's fibers and woven plastic products are used in conveyor belts, awnings, roofing, rope and, of course, tire cord and tires. The division employs more than 700 people and operates three manufacturing facilities in North America.

In contrast to its many successes, when Firestone detoured from rubber or automotive-related avenues in its path of diversification, the ventures often stalled. In 1971, the company announced the formation of Bank Firestone, Ltd., as a wholly owned subsidiary in Zurich Switzerland. After a four-year run, the banking operation was discontinued, the company conceding that "corporate efforts can be better utilized in other parts of the company more directly related to its primary business of mass producing and marketing broadly used products."

The lesson was quite simple—Firestone's strength revolved around its ingenuity in innovating within its core business around the world.

Staying Ahead of the Curve

Since the days of the first horseless carriage, Firestone has worked to stay ahead of the evolving performance needs of cars as well as the market needs of new generations of customers. Sometimes the innovations have been small incremental steps, with an occasional dramatic leap forward. Today as Bridgestone/Firestone, the company has introduced Ultimate Network of Intelligent Tire Technology, or UNI-T.® Developed during the '90s, this breakthrough technology helps maintain superior tire performance and grip in wet road conditions.

The company launched one of the first tires incorporating the technology, FT70c, with the largest advertising and promotional effort for any single product in its history. Advertising ran on ABC and NBC as well as magazines such as *Sports Illustrated.* To educate and generate enthusiasm at the store level, more than 500 Firestone retailers from across the country were whisked away to the company's proving grounds in Ft. Stockton, Texas, to participate in testing and evaluation.

The product was rolled out to the United States and reviews were favorable. *Sports Car International* raved about the new technology's improved traction, saying Bridgestone/Firestone "effected a quantum leap in wet weather adhesion." *Turbo & Hi-Tech Performance* said this major innovation was "much more than just a marketing gimmick."

The tire-buying public also responded with enthusiasm. The Firestone FT70c premium all-season tire with UNI-T quickly became the best-selling tire in the company's history—about 1.5 million tires sold in the first year—and one of the most successful launches in modern tire history.

During the late '90s, the company also incorporated other new Bridgestone technology into Bridgestone/Firestone products. First, it introduced an Extended Performance Compound that reduces hardening of the tire's rubber caused by friction heat. It also unveiled a Dual Layer Tread technology that uses two kinds of rubber to create a tread within the tread and greatly improve worn tire performance. These innovations, combined with UNI-T technology, produce UNI-T AQ™, which maintains a tire's performance in the wet, even as a tire wears.

"Our chief rivals have placed their primary focus on run-flat tire technology," said Shu Ishibashi, Bridgestone/Firestone vice president of consumer tire marketing. "While we've also introduced run-flat tires, our main goal has been developing a technology that is much more applicable in daily driving—one that addresses worn tire performance."

Each of Firestone's major innovations was created to meet a specific need. The road ahead remains the same for the company driven, in the words of its founder, to make the "best today, still better tomorrow."

Logo for Uni-T AQ and illustrations showing Uni-T AQ technology.

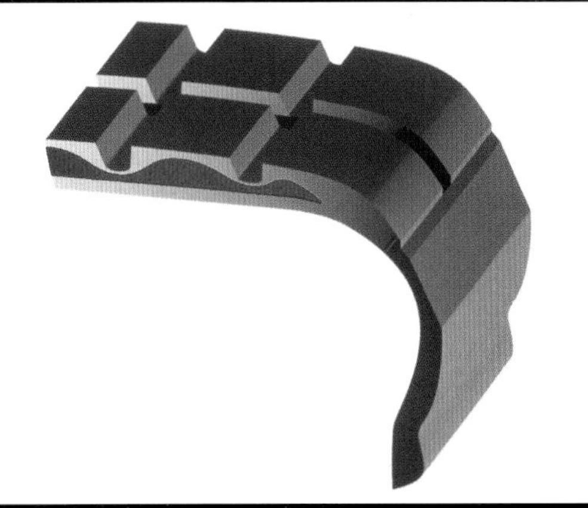

An illustration visually demonstrates Uni-T AQ's remarkable ability to extend worn tire performance. Essentially, as the original tread wears away, a second layer of higher grip rubber is exposed. **(Bridgestone/Firestone Collection)**

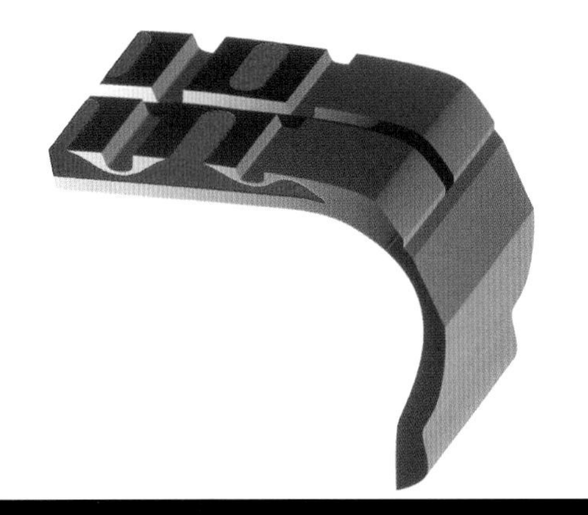

If I could tell you
Written for my daughter Elizabeth
Idabelle Fire
GEORGE-FOSTER-PEAB
Piano
The AIR'S Finest Program
The VOICE of Firestone
MILLIONS VISITED T
FIRESTONE FARM EXHI
FEATURING GROUND GI
TIRES AT THE GREAT LAK
EXPOSITION—MILLIO
MORE WILL SEE IT IN 1
could tell you
Firestone
mf poco rit.
See AIR BALLOON TIRES MADE AT THE FIRESTO
FACTORY AND EXHIBITION BUILDING WORLD'S F
Firestone Quality PRODUCTS

CHAPTER 4

VOICE IN THE MARKETPLACE

Rubber sings on the radio, fairs of the future and one-stop shops put Firestone on the map

On its journey through the 20th century, the Firestone name, like the diverse products it pioneered, has often ventured off the road and into people's homes to enrich their lives and fill their memories.

Through the years, Firestone has come to stand for something more than tires. The Firestone logo, a simple line of turn-of-the-century type, has become a piece of Americana, a symbol of quality and pride

Firestone's early venture into one-stop shopping in 1937 serves motoring needs with tires, tubes, batteries and radios as well as household tastes for toasters and waffle irons.
(Modern Tire Dealer Archive)

that is understood and appreciated around the world. Like the best of brands, it occupies a place in our collective minds and culture that makes it more than a mark.

The vehicles that carried Firestone to this place in our lives are as varied as our individual associations with the brand—a long-running radio show, a weekly television broadcast, lavish exhibits pointing us optimistically toward tomorrow, a favorite bicycle bought at a store carrying the Firestone name.

Building its brand, Firestone has taken the high road. That is not to suggest it hasn't run across its share of potholes while traveling that road. It is a matter of direction. It is simply to say that the Firestone century celebrates a brand that rose above physical products to be given a voice.

"...It is our hope and desire that these programs...will be a genuine source of entertainment in your home. If we make your half-hour with us each Monday evening a wholesome feature in your household, we will have realized the spirit which animates our radio program. As each week brings you a new Firestone program, we hope your enjoyment may bring us all even closer together and that the ***Voice of Firestone*** *may always have a friendly echo in your memory."*

– Harvey S. Firestone, on the first *Voice of Firestone* radio broadcast, December 3, 1928

Discounting with Dignity

By 1925, The Firestone Tire & Rubber Company had established a solid reputation for providing quality products, though not necessarily the least expensive ones. Company advertising pitched the "most miles per dollar" with Firestone tires. While others offered lower prices, it was important to Harvey S. Firestone to offer the best value through higher quality and longer wear. It was his merchandising mantra.

This strategy was threatened in the '20s by discounters and mail order tire merchants who flooded the market with cheap, low-mileage tires. Independent dealers of Firestone products felt the pinch of heightened competition based only on price.

Firestone decided to meet the competition with his own price cuts but, because he insisted on preserving the high product quality, he felt he could only do so by creating more outlets and reducing distribution costs. He reasoned that increasing the sales volume would allow him to lower prices, continue to provide superior quality, and keep his retailers profitable. To increase the number of Firestone dealers immediately and to experiment with expanded product lines, Firestone began supplementing the company's network of independent dealers with company-owned stores in 1925.

He also decided to sponsor a radio program featuring classical music—a masterstroke of marketing. What did classical music have to do with tires? Nothing. Firestone wasn't selling tires. It was selling quality.

Sponsoring the radio program not only associated Firestone products with something of comparable quality, but it also provided a completely new advertising vehicle for its products. Firestone's idea finally hit the air in 1928 as the *Voice of Firestone,* the most successful entertainment broadcast program of its time. It was a marketing milestone, a sponsorship of quality programming later imitated in *Texaco's Metropolitan Opera,* the *Hallmark Hall of Fame* series of television dramas, and the *Mobil Masterpiece Theater* series on public television. Firestone, however, was the first. More than any other show, the *Voice* demonstrated that high culture and popular culture, the art world and the auto world, could travel comfortably together.

Firestone greets the summer of '43 with a store full of fun for the car, home, work, and recreation.

(Bridgestone/Firestone Collection)

When Tires and Tenors Collide

On December 3, 1928, the first *Voice of Firestone* was broadcast on 41 radio stations. Thirty-five years passed before the program's unprecedented run ended. By that time, the program had been broadcast on thousands of stations and had launched or enhanced the careers of some of America's best known entertainers. Its string of broadcast industry

HARVEY AND IDABELLE: A LIFELONG DANCE

At a dance held at the home of a friend, Harvey was introduced to Idabelle Smith of Jackson, Michigan. In true Firestone fashion, he courted the fair-haired young lady from his buggy, indulging her with rides along the same boulevard he raced. They married in November 1895. Splurging to visit New York on their honeymoon, the young couple attended the theater, night after night. Their mutual love of fine music would one day be given a voice in the classic marketing initiative, the "Voice of Firestone."

(Bridgestone/Firestone Collection)

America never tires of Firestone, whether on the road or radio, and beginning with the late '40s, the Firestone Orchestra and the "Voice of Firestone" could be seen as well as heard on national television broadcasts. (Bridgestone/Firestone Collection)

firsts is the most extensive of any program—an impressive accomplishment for a program that featured classical and semi-classical music instead of popular tunes. Today, the program lives on, via videotape, recordings, and in the minds of many Americans over the age of 50 who recall it with warm regard.

As it ended its third decade, the program had the triple distinction of being the oldest coast-to-coast radio program on the air, the first musical program to be televised by a commercial sponsor and the first to be simulcast.

Many of the world's finest musical artists appeared on the *Voice of Firestone.* From this marvelous marketing platform America heard great featured orchestras such as Arthur Fiedler and the Boston Pops, the Philadelphia Symphony with Eugene Ormandy conducting, and Xaviar Cugat's Orchestra, which introduced many to the beat of South America. Eleanor Steiber was the musical artist perhaps most closely associated with the program. Other opera soloists who joined the *Voice* included Roberta Peters, soprano star of the Metropolitan Opera; the popular mezzo-soprano Rise Stevens;

matinee idol singer-actor Nelson Eddy; and Richard Rogers of Rogers and Hammerstein.

The format of the *Voice of Firestone* remained remarkably consistent over the years. Each broadcast typically featured four vocal numbers and three orchestral selections played by the 48-member Firestone Orchestra.

Commercial messages were tastefully intertwined with the music. Harvey S. Firestone, Sr., described the show as a "wholesome feature in your household." But its announcer also reminded listeners during the first *Voice of Firestone* broadcast that the company's tires "will give you more safety and more mileage than any tire of similar grade and price." He asked, "Why buy any other when you can buy a better tire from Firestone Service Dealers at the same price?"

The distinctively rich, mellow voice of Hugh James made these rather straightforward commercial pronouncements with a disarming warmth. He was hired from a list of 50 applicants and served as the program's announcer for many years, his voice deemed to be "more perfectly suited to the type of announcements and commercials made on the program than any other voice in radio and television."

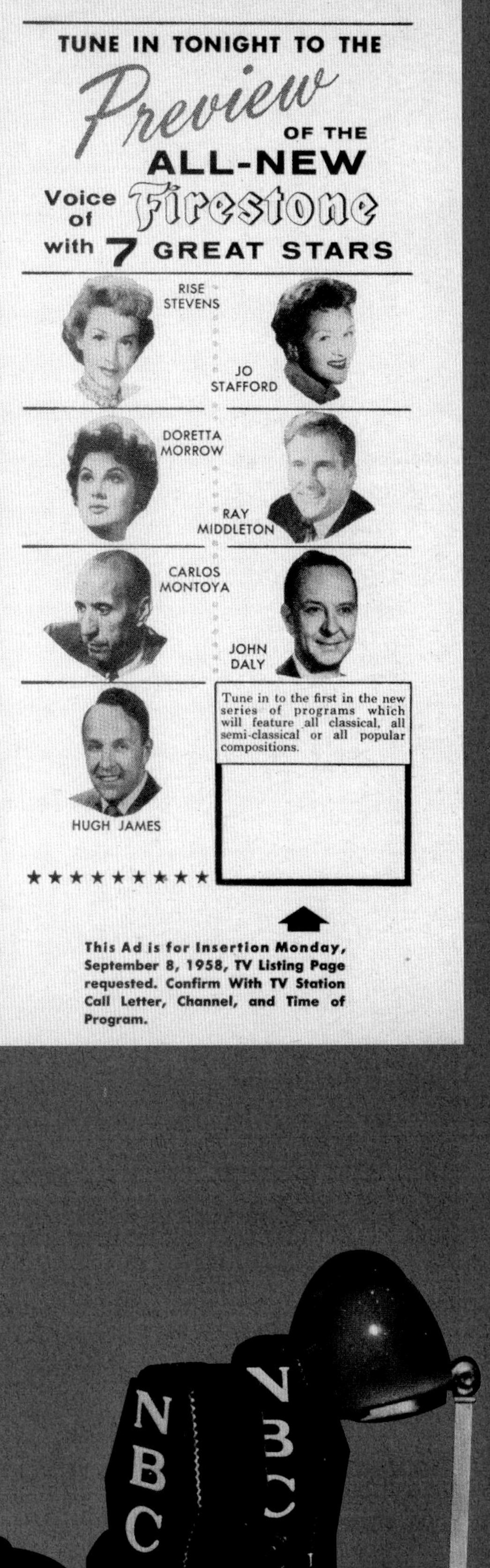

Newspaper ads touted the upcoming musical line-up as the "Voice of Firestone" got a second life as "the All-New Voice" on the ABC television network from 1954 to 1959.
(Bridgestone/Firestone Collection)

In the early '30s, culture and commerce comfortably co-exist on the "Voice of Firestone" with Harvey S. Firestone, Jr., romancing the tire industry in a series of talks on "The Story of Transportation."
(Bridgestone/Firestone Collection)

A Few Words from Our Sponsor

One way of capturing the history of a company is by recalling those lines and phrases it created over the years to present itself to the world. Here, then, is a slogan-by-slogan history of Firestone.

Let Us Introduce ~
"Mr. Most Miles Per Dollar"
the only Gum-Dipped tire made, giving greater safety, comfort and economy. He is a part of our service—we make him wear longer and your old tires help pay for him. How about an introduction?
SPENCER'S GARAGE
HIGGANUM, CONN.

"Most Miles Per Dollar" was a catchy promise popularized by Firestone when promoting the gum-dipped tire in the 1920s.
(Bridgestone/Firestone Collection)

FIRESTONE NON-SKID Harvey S. Firestone put these words on a piece of paper and told his designers to use the letters to make a tread design. They listened and using block lettering, about an inch and a quarter high, made the words "Firestone" and "Non-Skid" the actual tread pattern. For many years, Firestone could boast a unique tire that "left its name wherever it went."

WIN ON SUNDAY, SELL ON MONDAY Not exclusive to Firestone, it was used by Ford, Firestone, and others to underscore the importance of auto racing to their business. The power of this simple slogan was proven once again when Firestone returned to Indy car racing in 1995 and tire sales began climbing.

SHIP BY TRUCK Beginning in 1918, Harvey S. Firestone was instrumental in creating this movement which helped get the American trucking industry rolling.

MOST MILES PER DOLLAR A 1920s campaign line that captures Firestone's historic interest in quality and value.

PUT THE FARM ON RUBBER A crusade by Harvey S. Firestone to ease the life of farmers, whose rural upbringing he shared. Firestone was instrumental in replacing the steel-cleated wheels on farm tractors with low pressure all-rubber tires for greater comfort and a more economical operation.

EVERY FIRESTONE EMPLOYEE A SALESMAN For much of the 1930s, this message accompanied vacation pay checks. It reminded thousands of employees to spread the good word about the company and its products while they toured the country.

AMERICANS SHOULD PRODUCE THEIR OWN RUBBER A tag line created in 1922 by Harvey S. Firestone in his fight against international cartels and their attempts to control the output, distribution, and price of rubber. It prophetically warned of the predicament of the United States as it entered World War II—critically short of the rubber necessary to win while unable at the onset of the war to produce it.

WHERE THE RUBBER MEETS THE ROAD This trademark is one of the most recognized in the rubber industry and has been used as a memorable marketing piece to sell the Firestone brand and denote quality.

BEST TODAY...STILL BETTER TOMORROW The company's motto in the 1950s which evolved into **FIRESTONE: MAKING THE BEST TODAY STILL BETTER TOMORROW** in the 1960s.

GO TO THE FIELD Motto of Raymond Firestone who, as director of research and development, used it to underscore his belief that the field was the place to determine what needed to be done in tire design. He didn't want to rely on what engineers thought the public wanted or what they thought would do the job, but on what people said they wanted. Raymond became president in 1957.

THE NAME THAT'S KNOWN IS FIRESTONE Throughout the 1960s and 1970s, the slogan, which was turned into a jingle, and often combined with "Where the Rubber meets the Road," was based on the assertion made in a 1966 Rubber World article that said, "The Firestone Tire & Rubber Company is an international household name."

FIRESTONE TIRES FOR A NATION ON WHEELS This was a motto from the late 1970s.

BORN AT INDY, DRIVEN EVERYWHERE Since 1995, this tag line is used for the Firestone Firehawk Performance Tire. This slogan has since evolved to "Born at Indy, Performs Everywhere."

AMERICA'S TIRE SINCE 1900 Motto used in the 1990s by Bridgestone/Firestone underscores the importance of Firestone as a trusted and lasting piece of Americana.

LEADER IN THE FIELD The straightforward Firestone Agricultural Tire Company's slogan alludes to the company's market share.

A RACING LEGEND AT THE INDY 500 and **THE LEGEND RETURNS** Two slogans used in advertising as Firestone returned to Indy 500 competition in 1995.

BUILT TO STOP IN THE WET Slogan for the Firestone FT70c, a UNI-T® product that has become one of the best-selling tires in company history.

Dedication of the NBC Television Theater *Voice of Firestone* telecast of September 25, 1950. *The Voice* was an important element in the high cultural tone of early television.
(Bridgestone/Firestone Collection)

More important than selling tires was the program's power to present a prestige image. According to Harvey S. Firestone, Jr., the founder's son and company president from 1941 to 1948 and chairman through 1966, the program successfully emphasized "the quality of Firestone products and the high caliber of the Firestone organization."

Along with benefiting Firestone, the program was of inestimable value to the music it played and the musicians who played it.

"One reason opera is flourishing in the United States today is a program called the *Voice of Firestone*," said Joseph McLellan, music critic for the *Washington Post*. "No causal connection can be firmly established, but it is interesting that so many American opera companies were started in the postwar years when this program was going out nationwide and propagandizing the opera, intensely, to a mass audience."

The combination of high culture and popular attention drew awards as well as a stack of positive reviews. Among its many awards, in 1956, the program earned the George Foster Peabody Radio-Television Award, one of the highest honors in the field of entertainment. It cited the *Voice of Firestone* for the "highest sensitivity not only in the matter of superb program standards but also in its understanding of advertising proprieties."

The Romancing of Rubber

Never has one program accomplished so many purposes. The music and advertising were supplemented by "short talks" given by Firestone, his sons, or company officials. In some cases, these talks served to present "the romance and the drama of the rubber industry." In others, the message was more political, with a strong appeal to patriotism.

The show also encouraged support for Firestone-favored charities, such as the Boy Scouts, Future Farmers of America, National 4H Clubs, Red Cross, and the USO.

Along with the Firestone sons' involvement in producing the program, Harvey S. Firestone, Sr.'s wife, Idabelle, played an important role. Her songs, "If I Could Tell You" and "In my Garden" opened and closed each program.

If I could tell you
Of my devotion
If I could pledge all my love so true.
Then my confession
Would find expression
In all the music my heart sings to you.

Year in and year out, this song began the show, sung by a guest performer before they turned to their own songs.

In addition to Idabelle, other Firestone family members contributed musically to the program. Elizabeth Firestone, a young composer and pianist and the daughter of Mr. and Mrs. Harvey S. Firestone, Jr., debuted on the *Voice of Firestone* March 20, 1950.

Famous First a Fluke

Most of Firestone's famed firsts were discovered and planned. However, there was one notable exception.

On March 22, 1948, when the Firestone Orchestra moved into Studio 8-H to produce its weekly radio program, it found the room still set for the previous day's NBC telecast of a musical program featuring Toscanini. On the

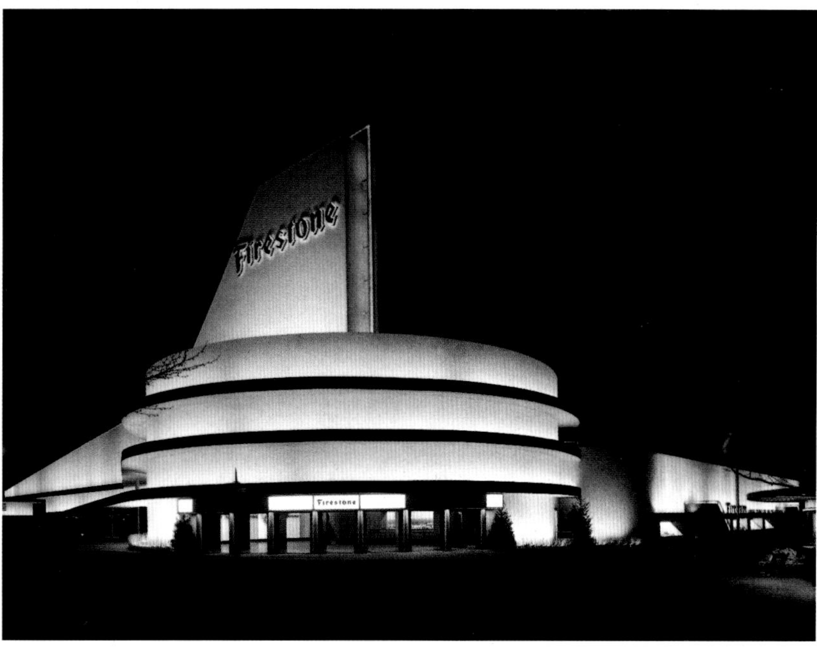

The Firestone Pavilion at the 1939-40 New York World's Fair was a striking example of modern architecture, featuring a great rotunda entrance and 100-foot fin tower. Inside the pavilion was a modern tire factory that rolled out a finished tire every four minutes.
(Bridgestone/Firestone Collection)

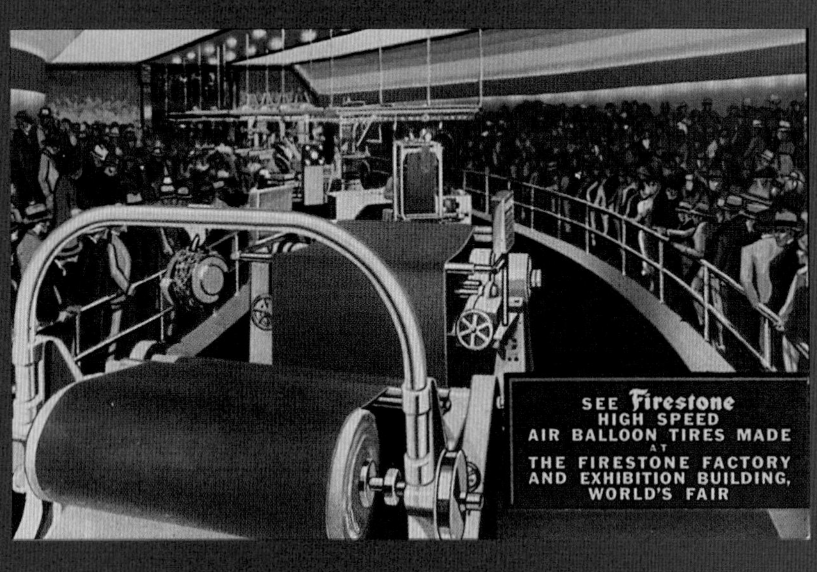

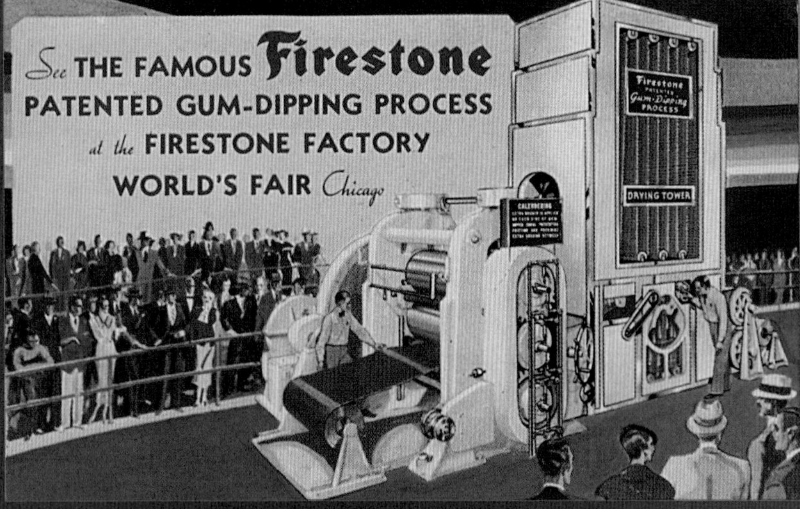

spur of the moment, Firestone decided to telecast the evening's show as well as broadcast it on the radio. When the program aired, the company became the first to telecast a commercially sponsored musical program and the first company to sponsor a commercial simulcast on AM, FM, television, and short wave.

Firestone
THE FIRESTONE SINGING COLOR FOUNTAIN AND MULTI-PLANE SHADOW SIGN. ONLY INSTALLATIONS OF THEIR KIND IN THE WORLD. A CENTURY OF PROGRESS.

Firestone soon discovered that simulcasting required a little bit of fine tuning. In radio, people seldom noticed how many of the same guest artists performed week after week. But the television audience complained about seeing the same faces too frequently so, in 1950, the program began a policy of scheduling an artist no more than four times a year.

The Voice Continues to Be Heard

In 1954, NBC canceled the program, saying it could no longer provide a suitable broadcast time. Millions of loyal listeners were stunned and thousands of them flooded the network, local stations, and the Firestone company with letters, telegrams, and phone calls. People who had long taken the program for granted protested its demise.

A series of postcards from the 1933 Century of Progress World's Fair in Chicago illustrates the highlights of the Firestone Factory and Exhibition Building, including a modern tire-making demonstration, gum-dipping and the colorful splash of the Firestone Singing Color Fountain.

(Bridgestone/Firestone Collection)

Firestone learned from the outcry the power of the listener loyalty it had created. Research conducted following the announcement showed the average *Voice* listener stayed loyal to the program for 10 to 12 years while other shows held their attention only two or three years. Even more amazing for a classical music program was its popularity among entire families, children as well as parents. Beginning with the very first program in 1928, Harvey S. Firestone said he wanted a vehicle to "bring us all even closer together."

His *Voice* had lived up to those dreams.

CBS seized the opportunity to pick up the popular program and featured Arthur Fiedler as the principal conductor. The *Voice of Firestone* was heard throughout the land another nine years. Until June 16, 1963, when the final curtain was drawn, the program remained true to its original plan of providing the best in quality entertainment. Fortunately, what many have regarded as one of our national treasures is preserved in 32 years of radio and television broadcast tapes and 1,639 original instrumental and vocal arrangements donated to the New England Conservatory of Music.

Today, almost 40 years since the *Voice* was silenced on the airwaves, it's still drawing rave reviews. With grants from the Firestone family, the conservatory began releasing the programs in early 1989 for a new generation of Americans. With the first release of 40 videotapes, The *New York Times* said that "the 'Firestone' vocal roster was an impressive one. From an era far richer than our own in commanding voices, many of the finest are on parade here." The *Dallas Morning News* wrote on September 10, 1990, "there is gold in these tapes" while that same year the *Seattle Post Intelligencer* noted that many baby-boomers got their first exposure to serious art through these shows.

Carrying on the legacy of The Firestone Tire & Rubber Company founded by their father, the five Firestone brothers inspect the site of the huge exhibit building at the 1939-40 New York World's Fair. Roger, Raymond, Harvey, Jr., Russell, and Leonard all wear black armbands in honor of their recently deceased father.

(University of Akron Archives – Firestone Collection)

From Culture to Agriculture

The marketing genius that created the *Voice of Firestone* didn't try to reinvent the wheel when it began looking for a way to touch other audiences. As the company became a leading force in rubberizing the farm with products like the Firestone Ground Grip Tire, it needed a way to get its message into the farmhouse. So in 1937, it began broadcasting the Firestone *Voice of the Farm*, heard from coast-to-coast during the noon hour over a nationwide radio network of 76 leading stations.

The new show featured famous agricultural commentator Everett Mitchell's interviews with farming experts. Farmers came in for lunch and listened to the *Voice* as it addressed important agricultural issues. The bond between Firestone and the farmer grew.

"[*Voice of the Farm*] enjoys unprecedented popularity with dealers. It has done much to establish a closer relationship between your company and farmers everywhere," noted a 1938 company document to dealers.

A deluge of letters for more information and reprints of interviews greeted each show.

The
MASTERPIECE
of TIRE
CONSTRUCTION

SELECTED BY

Surely it is a tribute to outstanding qualit
service to again be selected by A Centu
Progress to represent the Rubber Industry a
World's Fair. The Firestone Factory and Exhi
Building and the scientific rubber exhibit
Hall of Science have been remodeled
enlarged to include many new instructive fea

See how rubber is gathered from the tre
the Firestone Plantation in Liberia, Africa,
it is mixed in the huge massing machine. Se
the millions of cotton fibers in Firestone high

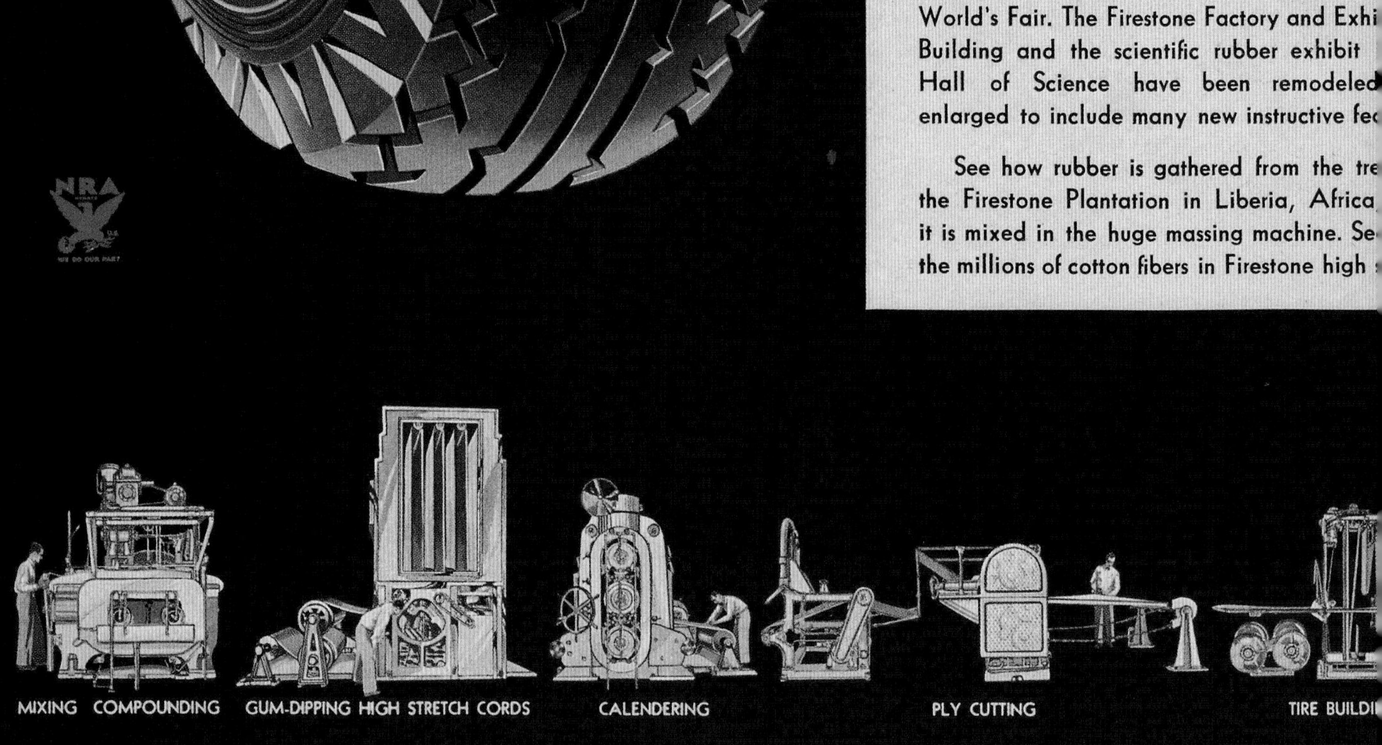

MIXING COMPOUNDING

GUM-DIPPING HIGH STRETCH CORDS

CALENDERING

PLY CUTTING

TIRE BUILDI

Firestone

ENTURY OF PROGRESS FOR 1934

s are automatically soaked and coated with liquid rubber he Firestone patented process of Gum-Dipping, providing ter strength, safety and blowout protection; how the new tone Low Pressure Air Balloon tire is made, from the ng of the rubber to the finished tire, as illustrated below.

See the demonstrations of extra power and long life in stone Batteries and Spark Plugs, and the extra braking iency of Firestone Brake Linings, all developed by tone engineers and manufactured in Firestone factories.

See the dynamic exhibits of the new Firestone Low Pressure Tractor Tires, Wheels and Rims. Visit the Singing Color Fountains in the Firestone gardens—concerts every day and night—the only spectacle of its kind in the world.

Before you motor to the Fair have the Firestone Service Dealer or Service Store in your community inspect your tires, test your brakes, battery and spark plugs, that you may have an enjoyable and trouble-free trip. There is no charge for this service.

Listen to Lawrence Tibbett or Richard Crooks and Harvey Firestone, Jr., every Monday night—N.B.C. Network

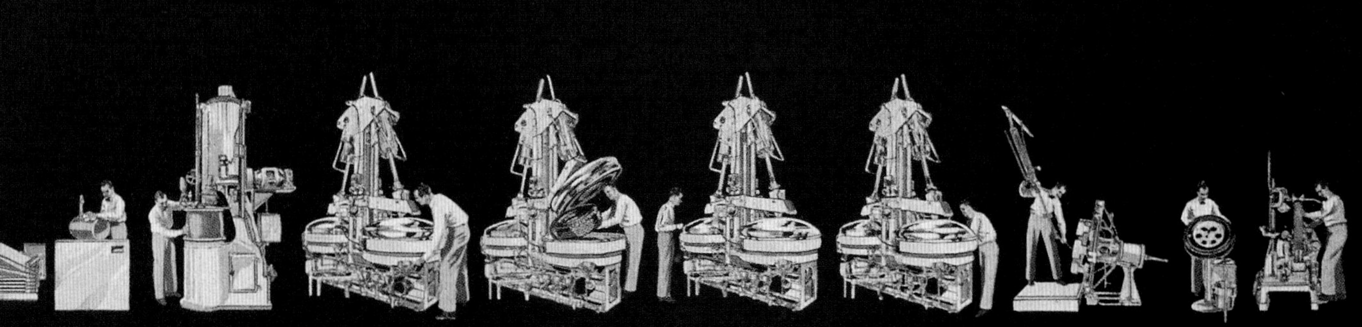

New York Mayor Fiorello LaGuardia takes part in the dedication of the Firestone Tire & Rubber Company building at the New York World's Fair by driving rivets into the structure beam. Joining the mayor are (left to right) Roger S. Firestone; project construction worker; Harvey S. Firestone, Jr.; John W. Thomas, president of the company; and Harold A. Flanigan, vice president of the Fair Corporation.
(University of Akron Archives – Firestone Collection)

Before the eyes of New York World's Fair-goers, Firestone builds the tire of tomorrow, from raw rubber to finished product.
(Bridgestone/Firestone Collection)

(Previous page) A 1934 Firestone ad celebrates the Century of Progress World's Fair in Chicago as well as "The Masterpiece of Tire Construction."
(Bridgestone/Firestone Collection)

This unprecedented demand for information led to the formation of the Firestone Farm Service Bureau, a library and clearinghouse for agricultural advice. Within a few months of the bureau's opening, it sent out more than 1.5 million pieces of mail to farmers. So popular was the service, Firestone constructed a special bureau headquarters at the New York World's Fair in 1939.

The Firestone Tire & Rubber Company exhibited a flair for showmanship. It was a successful company that along the road had discovered its voice and had something to say. The great world's fairs and expositions that marked the beginning of the century gave the company a global platform from which to speak. At the fairs, Firestone took the forefront with an awe-inspiring pavilion and displays. If a plain black tire was simplicity itself, the way it was presented to the world by Firestone was colorful and compelling.

More than 10 million people visited the Firestone Factory and Exhibition Building at the 1933 Century of Progress World's Fair in Chicago. There they witnessed firsthand the making of Firestone tires—from gum-dipping the cords to the tire's final finishing—in an immaculate factory, featuring gleaming chromium-plated machines.

The 1936 Great Lakes Exposition in Cleveland was closer to home. Along with a singing fountain and other proven crowd pleasers, this exhibit presented an incredible indoor farm complete with animals and was worked by a farmer and milkmaid using farm implements from the Firestone Homestead in Columbiana.

On the eve of World War II, Firestone put on another great show at the 1939-40 New York World's Fair in Flushing Meadows. The company's exhibit combined a working farm and factory. In keeping with the fair's futuristic theme—"World of Tomorrow"—Firestone made history on August 3, 1940, when its pavilion factory demonstrated to the public how tires were crafted from synthetic rubber. It was a fitting centerpiece for a company and country that would soon be engaged in a battle to heighten synthetic rubber production so critical to the final outcome of World War II.

(Bridgestone/Firestone Collection)

One-Stop Shopping Proves Popular

While culture and agriculture-oriented radio and television broadcasts and awe-inspiring fair displays made people feel closer to the company emotionally, Firestone's innovative retail ideas put the company in touch with customers by bringing it closer to them geographically.

As mentioned earlier in the chapter, Harvey S. Firestone decided to open company-owned retail stores in order to increase retail distribution. There was, however, another powerful marketing motive.

In an increasingly competitive marketplace, Firestone believed its independent dealers might not survive if they only offered tires. Even adding a gasoline pump and a few automotive accessories might not mean the difference between success and failure. The company had to help transform tire dealers into retailers. It envisioned a one-stop shop for all a customer's car needs so that the Firestone name was synonymous with car care and convenience. The challenge, of course, was finding the right merchandise and presentation to build this one-stop operation and convincing independent retailers the strategy worked. Rather than tell them, it would show them.

In 1925, Firestone opened four company-owned stores as a marketing laboratory for its new ideas. The decision proved to be another important marketing move.

"Our policy of cooperating with our dealers in establishing One-Stop Service Stores is proving very successful as it gives the car owner a standard and economical service on tires, tubes, batteries, gasoline, oil, brake linings, rims, and other automobile accessories," Firestone reported. "These modern service stores are widely distributed throughout the country, and we're planning to increase them in cooperation with our dealers as fast as conditions warrant."

Remarkably, as Firestone added company-owned stores, the number of independent dealers grew. As it added more retail products and services, it added more independent dealers. At a time when the economic uncertainty of the Great Depression was forcing thousands of businesses to close, Firestone stores were springing up across the country. Drawing from what it learned at the store level helped the company survive the Depression. In 1937, it opened its third American manufacturing plant and ended the year with record sales of $156,823,094.

At the time of Harvey S. Firestone's death in 1938, the network of company stores stood at 575, each handling more than 2,200 products. This was in addition to the huge network of independent Firestone dealers. Surviving the rocky road of economic depression, Firestone was ready to roll into the '40s and the business roadblocks presented by war.

When World War II broke out and the government restricted the sale of rubber goods, it

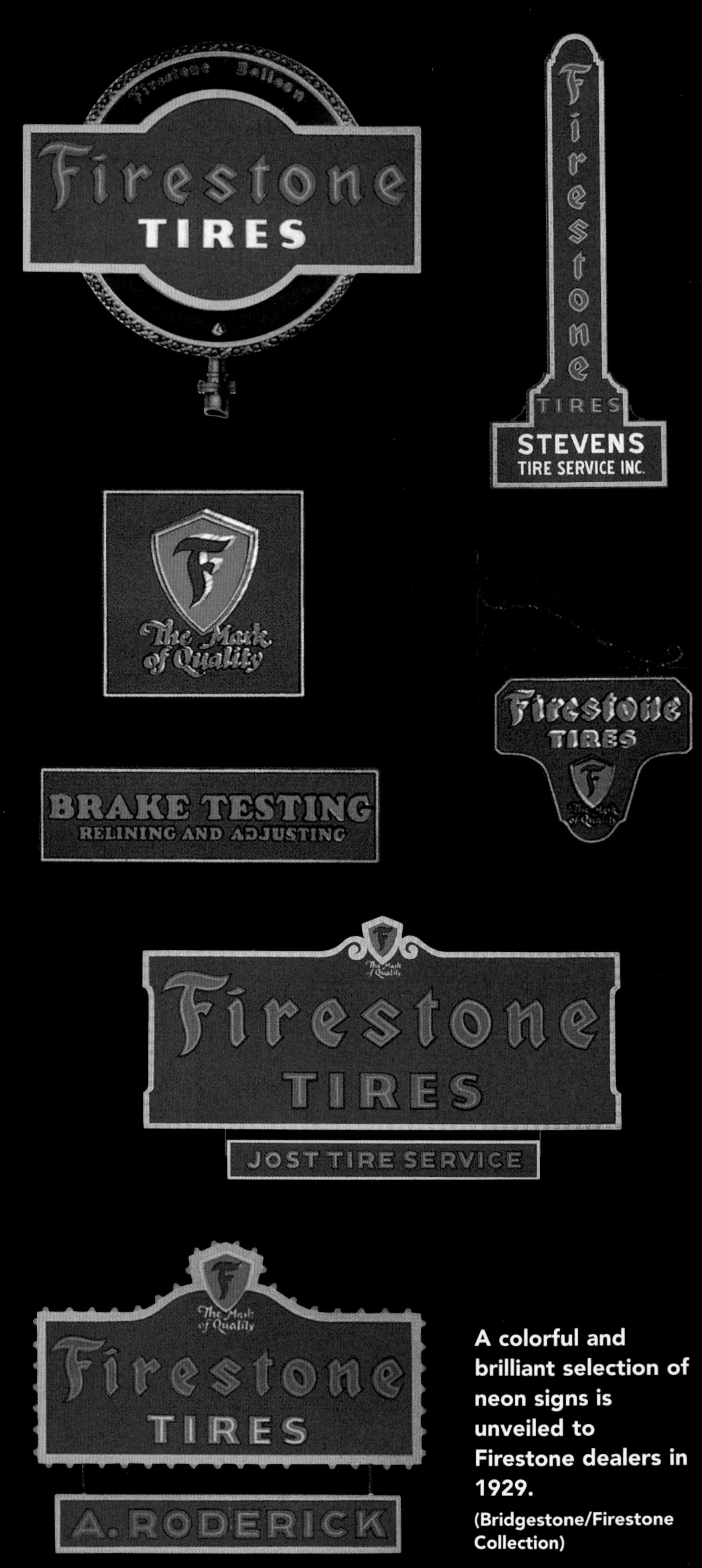

A colorful and brilliant selection of neon signs is unveiled to Firestone dealers in 1929.
(Bridgestone/Firestone Collection)

The role of the dealer, whether a wholesale, independent, mass merchandise or company store, has always been pivotal to the sales, improvement and success of Firestone Tires. Today's modern tire dealerships use advanced computer technology to help savvy consumers make tire selections.
(Bridgestone/Firestone Collection

could have been the end of the road for Firestone dealers—or any tire dealer—dependent solely upon the tire or rubber business. Firestone was ready. The number of consumer goods sold in the company stores and many of its independent dealers had grown. The stores weren't solely dependent on the sale of tires and rubber goods. Instead, they became wartime general stores detouring from automotive products to offer dinner plates and glassware, paints and wallpaper, work and dress clothing, phonograph records, farm and garden supplies, toys and games, and many other household items.

Firestone supported its dealers by testing products suitable for sale in their stores and by providing advertising support. The rewards to the company came rolling in at the war's close when a strong dealer network stood ready for the boom of a postwar economy and the return to an unrestricted market for automotive products.

By 1950, Firestone stores carried more than 4,000 different items, including bicycles, major appliances, and radios. The company celebrated its 50th anniversary with a worldwide distribution of 65,000 independent dealers and 725 company-owned stores.

Today, Bridgestone/Firestone's retail division continues to shine, operating more than 1,500 company-owned stores as Firestone Tire & Service Centers, Expert Tire, Tire Station, and Mark Morris retail centers. Its simple mission "to make car care easier for our customers" has made it the largest automotive service and repair company in the United States.

In addition, the company continues to grow its business in partnership with its independent dealers through initiatives like its Affiliated Dealers program and TireStarz.

Ship by Truck
DIVISION 40
DIVISION 41
ARMY PARTY ST
NEAR COLUMB
President and Mrs. Fir
Entertain Motor Convoy
Old Homestead
Firestone
WORLD
ATLAS
ONDAY BIG DAY
FOR FIRESTONE
40 pages
DOUBLE PAGE
MAPS
Full Color
Firestone Plantat
Harbel Gro
Liberia
Firestone vs. Cincin
CHICAGO NEEDS YOU IN THE WORLD SERIES KID!
OH YOU SWEET PATOOTIE!
Better
Community
Movement
50 YEARS OF Firestone SERVICE 1900-1950
Leroy Sadler

BUILDING A BETTER WORLD

5

Good roads, the great wars, and a transcontinental hike with Ike show Firestone's commitment to its country

Service and innovation—the two aren't such distant ideas. They move down parallel paths. Both work to fulfill a need. Both force us to look at the big picture, to look beyond the immediate to envision something better. Both, in spite of everything, share a wonderful sense of optimism—a belief that we can improve the world around us. Service, like innovation, has played a pivotal role in Firestone's first century

Harvey S. Firestone became a powerful voice for the "Ship by Truck" movement, as seen in this 1919 Saturday Evening Post ad. The visionary saw the opportunity to bolster the fledgling trucking industry and create public interest in improving the nation's roadways. (University of Akron Archives – Firestone Collection)

"Ship by Truck"

—the traffic motto of today and the future

By Harvey S. Firestone
President, Firestone Tire & Rubber Co.

THE necessities of war brought home to us the importance of the motor truck. When the French line stood at the Marne, the truck began to receive the recognition it deserved.

War, in that emergency, taught us overnight an industrial lesson that we would otherwise have taken years to learn. People realized, all at once, that the motor truck was essential and vital in our transportation, and therefore a basic part of our living.

Like good roads, motor trucking should interest every man, woman or child. Both are basic elements in lowering the cost of distribution, saving products now wasted, opening up resources heretofore untapped.

The truck is ready and able to shoulder burdens the railroads cannot carry and to leave them free for responsibilities too long deferred and delayed.

It is a time for principals to confer—a time for them to co-operate. The traffic situation is one of greatest significance. Our future industrial growth depends largely upon the assistance rendered the railroads by trucks in speeding up freight movement. Communities which are not served by the railroads find in the truck the means for their rapid development.

"Ship by truck."

Let us make this the slogan of a new business era.

Truck lines already stream out from city to city, from distributing centers to the surrounding towns, hamlets and rural districts. Use the truck arteries. You'll serve yourself and the public. You'll relieve the railroads of a part of the overwhelming demands now being made upon them.

The truck is the one satisfactory solution to the difficulties of short-haul freight. The hundred-mile radius belongs to the truck. But the truck has not stopped there. Its future is restricted only by the extent of good roads and systematic schedules.

"Ship by truck."

You'll save and serve. Pass the word on to your traffic department. Take it up with your business associates. Speak of it to others in your industry.

Whether it's your truck or one belonging to a truck transport company—

"Ship by truck."

Speed traffic; aid the railroads to give the country a freighting system that can cope with the rapid growth of industry. Get in line with the future trend of transportation.

"Ship by truck."

"Every useful occupation is ample opportunity for service. The happiest men in the world are those who are making their jobs mean more than simply an endless routine of work and wages. The whole structure of business is making and doing useful things for others. That is service."

– Harvey S. Firestone

of success. Just as the company came to stand for more than merely tires in terms of products, its philosophy traveled beyond the betterment of the company to include the greater good of the globe. From improving the nation's roadways to promoting more energy-efficient modes of transportation, from ridding the world of rubber cartels to joining the fight to keep it free, Firestone's history of service stretches the length and breadth of the 20th century, embracing some of the era's most compelling causes.

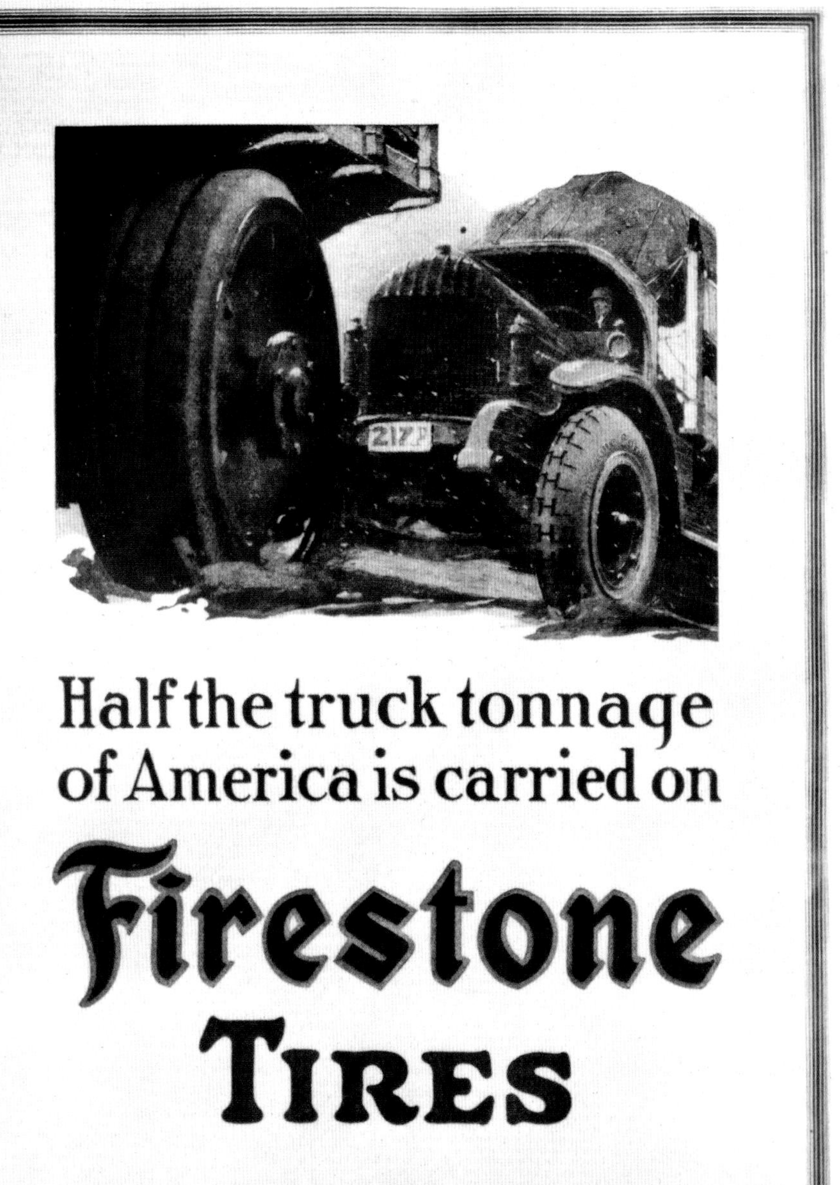

Half the truck tonnage
of America is carried on
Firestone
TIRES

Good Roads Getting Rolling

As much as Harvey S. Firestone loved to explore the rutted backroads of America with his famous friends, he knew that if the nation were to move forward, the quaint byways would have to give way to a national system of highways. All of his life, Firestone believed the growth of America depended upon expanded transportation and supported any campaign that promoted the idea.

Along with other industrialists, Firestone supported the Lincoln Highway Association when it organized in 1913 to create the thoroughfare which was the premier, albeit unfinished, highway of its era. He was also a staunch proponent of the "Good Roads" movement.

Even before the turn of the century and the advent of the automobile, millions of bicyclists derided the nation's roads as one colorful contemporary slogan suggested—"Wholly unclassable, almost impassable, scarcely jackassable!" Prior to 1908, only 7 percent of the nation's rural roads had any kind of surfacing. And so the "Good Roads" movement was born. When the horseless carriage sputtered into history, the "Good Roads" movement became a formidable federation of regional political organizations that, as early as 1912, urged the improvement of roads, primarily in rural areas. "Good Roads" brought together groups as diverse as the fledgling American Automobile Association, the National Grange, and the National Association of Rural Letter Carriers. All across America, from Maine to California, local "Good Roads" groups formed and awakened the nation to the need for federal involvement in highway transportation.

It worked. In the middle of 1916, President Woodrow Wilson signed the first federal law to establish a nationwide system of interstate highways. There was still, however, more to be done. Ironically, it would take the aftershocks of World War I to further the cause of the country's embattled roadways.

One veteran vehicle of the "Ship by Truck" movement boasts where it's been to further the cause. **(Modern Tire Dealer Archives)**

Trucks line up in the staging area for the big "Ship by Truck" rally that would roll through the Twin Cities and into the St. Paul state fairgrounds on September 1, 1919. More than 500,000 would witness this impressive display.
(University of Akron Archives – Firestone Collection)

Steering the Truck Movement

The Great War provided proof of the value of trucks. At the Battle of Verdun, the Allies used 8,000 trucks to ferry troops and supplies to the front. In the United States, 30,000 trucks moved supplies to Eastern ports for shipment to American troops and our Allies in France.

When the war ended, bad roads not only presented a road block to the postwar demand for more goods, but also were an obstacle for the burgeoning motortruck makers. With production geared up for the war effort, trucks rolled off the assembly lines in greater numbers. But where were the roads to carry them?

Harvey S. Firestone and his fellow tiremakers worried, along with truck manufacturers, that the new industry would collapse if something wasn't done. Firestone believed a massive campaign to sell trucks to the nation's shippers, manufacturers, farmers, and consumers could accomplish two purposes—bolster the truck industry and heighten the demand for more and better roads.

In 1918, Firestone inaugurated the successful "Ship by Truck" campaign which led to the development of the nation's powerful trucking industry. "Ship by Truck" was a companion to the "Good Roads" movement and involved many of the same movers. It had, however, the targeted goal of boosting the sale and use of freight-hauling trucks by building better highways.

Cross-Country Caravan

World War I's wake produced another wave of interest in the nation's roadways as part of a dramatic cross-country military maneuver. In 1919, an Army convoy rolled across America on a journey to determine if military equipment could motor from coast-to-coast on the country's deplorable roads. The caravan consisted of an odd assortment of vehicles, including 34 heavy trucks, four light trucks, two machine shop vehicles, one blacksmith shop truck, one wrecker, two trucks loaded with spare parts, one gasoline and two water tankers, one searchlight vehicle, four kitchen trailers, eight touring cars, one reconnaissance car, two staff cars, five sidecar motorcycles, four single-seat motorcycles, and one tractor that frequently was used to pull the other vehicles out of the typical roadway mud.

Many of the 3,251 miles the caravan traveled were little more than dirt trails covered with mud or sand. On parts of the trip, travelers inched along treacherous mountain paths. Even the Lincoln Highway—the nation's finest—was difficult to traverse. In many cases, roads and bridges required repairs or reinforcement before the convoy could proceed. Equipment failures were frequent and difficult to fix.

"Extreme heat, low-hanging clouds of alkali dust, two-feet of sand up the wheel hubs and deplorable desert trails, numerous hidden chuck holes, and unusual dry conditions as the result of no rain for four months, and no material save sagebrush with which to build trails, were some of the trials the convoy by sheer grit and the American spirit of stick-to-itiveness managed to overcome," wrote one reporter traveling with the caravan. "The men were kept busy digging wheels out of holes and jacking trucks up into the air for clearing out and minor repairs."

Stories about the convoy filled the front pages. Every wrecked bridge and washed-out road was newsworthy and informed all Americans of the state of the nation's roadways.

By the time the convoy reached San Francisco, it had passed through some 350 communities. Even though the route purposefully avoided large cities, an estimated three million people witnessed the trucks roll past. When they heard the caravan was coming, townspeople gathered to greet the soldiers, waving flags and serving them snacks of coffee, lemonade, sandwiches and homemade pie. The town fathers made patriotic speeches in honor of their guests and the soldiers would join the locals at picnics or street dances, allowing the men a chance to mix with the young ladies from the farms and small towns.

One of the small towns the convoy visited was Columbiana, Ohio.

Part of the "Firestone Outfit" participating in the U.S. Army Transcontinental Motor Convoy of July-September 1919. Along the route, the convoy visited local Firestone dealers. Firestone used every opportunity to illustrate the usefulness of trucks to a nation that had come to rely on rail. When a switchman's strike crippled the railroads in 1920, Firestone employed trucks to support its dealers with their tire inventories.

(Modern Tire Dealer Archives)

Ike's Inspiration

When Harvey S. Firestone, Sr., heard about the dusty caravan crossing the country, he naturally invited all 300 people and 70 vehicles to the family's ancestral home for Sunday dinner. Following a meal set on the grounds beneath the cover of raised tent canopies, the group was treated to a concert with an appropriate musical program that included "Onward Christian Soldiers" and "Keep the Home Fires Burning."

It was a memorable evening. Especially to one member of the military convoy, a 28-year-old lieutenant colonel in the tank corps named Dwight David Eisenhower or "Ike." It was another instance where a trip and an unexpected friendship made by Firestone advanced the cause of the automobile.

Many years later, Ike wrote to Harvey Firestone, Jr., that the visit to Columbiana was still "memorable." It was the transcontinental caravan that Eisenhower said "started him thinking" about the value of good roads. While on the trip, the seed of an idea for an extensive system of highways first took root in his mind. It bloomed 37 years later when, as President of the United States, Eisenhower led the legislative crusade for the Interstate Highway System we know today.

In 1919, a U.S. Army convoy rumbled across America, often mired in mud and illustrating the deplorable state of the nation's roadways. A tractor was brought on the transcontinental journey to pull the other vehicles out of the mud.

(Russ Vitale Photography)

Along with the obvious lesson that the nation needed better roads, other practical insights emerged from the grueling 63-day experiment, such as the fact that pneumatic tires for trucks and cars worked far better than solid ones. Firestone dramatically pointed this out. He added two trucks to the caravan when it reached Akron. The new vehicles featured Firestone pneumatic tires rather than the solid rubber tires used by the Army trucks. While the Army vehicles' tires frequently bogged down in the mud and sand, Firestone's tires rode along with little difficulty.

One for the Road

Firestone continued its advocacy for road safety, economic efficiency, and the freedom of mobility long after the Eisenhower caravan passed into history.

During the 1920s, the company sponsored a national "Good Roads" essay contest to underscore the effect of good roads upon the "moral, religious, and educational advancement of the country." The winner of the first four-year college scholarship was Katherine Butterfield of Weiser, Idaho, who was notified of her selection by President Warren Harding in front of the newsreel cameras. By 1925, almost $1 billion a year was spent on road building. The same schoolchildren who wrote in favor of roads grew up to enjoy the modern highways envisioned in their essays.

In 1932, Firestone joined Alfred P. Sloan, Jr., president of General Motors, to incorporate the National Highway Users Conference. The organization's stated purpose was to "get the farmers out of the mud." By now, everyone knew the nation's roads were in wretched condition and something had to be done.

In 1956, H. D. Tompkins, a Firestone vice president who headed the Inter-Industry Highway Safety Committee, announced the company's support for the Boggs Bill that created the gas tax pay-as-you-go financing mechanism that finally made the Interstate

On July 13, 1919, the first Trans-Continental Motor Convoy pauses on its 3,251-mile journey to visit the home of Harvey S. Firestone. Firestone, at left, greets a member of the convoy with a handshake, while on the far right stands a young Lt. Col. named Dwight David Eisenhower. Later, when Eisenhower became President, he would remember the grueling journey and champion the interstate system.
(University of Akron Archives – Firestone Collection)

This 1928 ad underscores the importance of Firestone's vertical integration of the tire-making process. By operating its own rubber plantations in Liberia, the company freed itself from foreign control of rubber, inflated pricing and raw material shortages.
(Bridgestone/Firestone Collection)

Highway System possible. The interstate system—the ultimate outcome of Firestone's work on behalf of "Good Roads" and "Ship by Truck"—has made America the most mobile nation in the world. Its 42,000 miles of multi-laned divided highways with controlled interchanges is a tribute to Firestone and the many others who recognized the urgent need for better roads.

Today, in keeping with its founder's push for better roads, Bridgestone/Firestone continues to work for safety on the roads by developing new tire technology. In fact, Bridgestone truck tire casings have been voted the most durable since 1985, providing a higher level of highway safety for trucks and the drivers with whom they share the road.

Drawing from his rural roots, Firestone took a personal interest in improving the life of farmers. The seed planted by the founder has resulted in a tradition of leadership in the agricultural tire industry.
(Bridgestone/Firestone Collection)

Inflated Rubber Poses Problem

Highways weren't the only routes Firestone sought to smooth and free from obstacles. It also succeeded in removing roadblocks thrown up by a British rubber cartel.

In the early days of rubber production, England controlled the price of the rubber

Harvey S. Firestone takes time away from Akron to drive a steel-wheeled tractor at his boyhood home in Columbiana. Personal experience with the unforgiving metal wheels convinced him that rubber tires would greatly improve the farmers' way of life. Flanking Harvey are his sons, Leonard and Raymond Firestone. When shown this picture 42 years later in 1968, Raymond C. Firestone, Chairman of the Board, recalled, "I can tell you that the steel wheels give you a most uncomfortable ride. The tractor's pounding and vibration left the driver exhausted at the end of the day." (Modern Tire Dealer Archives)

supply grown in their colonies. In November 1922, Britain began inflating rubber prices with the aid of the Stevenson Rubber Restriction Act.

Firestone felt the tire and automobile industries were imperiled by this foreign monopoly. He believed that the American consumer shouldn't be forced to pay more for tires and new cars because of a political scheme that was driving higher prices. In 1922, Firestone began an effort to alert the industry and the nation to this cartel-like grip on the supply and price of rubber. He promoted the campaign with advertising that proclaimed "Americans should produce their own rubber."

In 1926, after watching the price of rubber escalate from about 14 cents a pound to more than $1.23, Firestone changed words into deeds and began producing his own rubber. The company negotiated a lease of jungle acreage from the Liberian government in West Africa and transformed it into a thriving rubber plantation.

Today, covering 188 square miles, the Firestone plantation in Harbel, Liberia, is the largest single rubber plantation in the world. Along with supplying the globe with natural rubber, it serves the Harbel area with schools, churches, and community organizations.

Where the Rubber Meets the Row

No matter how far new technology and economic success have taken the company from its rural upbringing, Firestone has remained mindful of its roots.

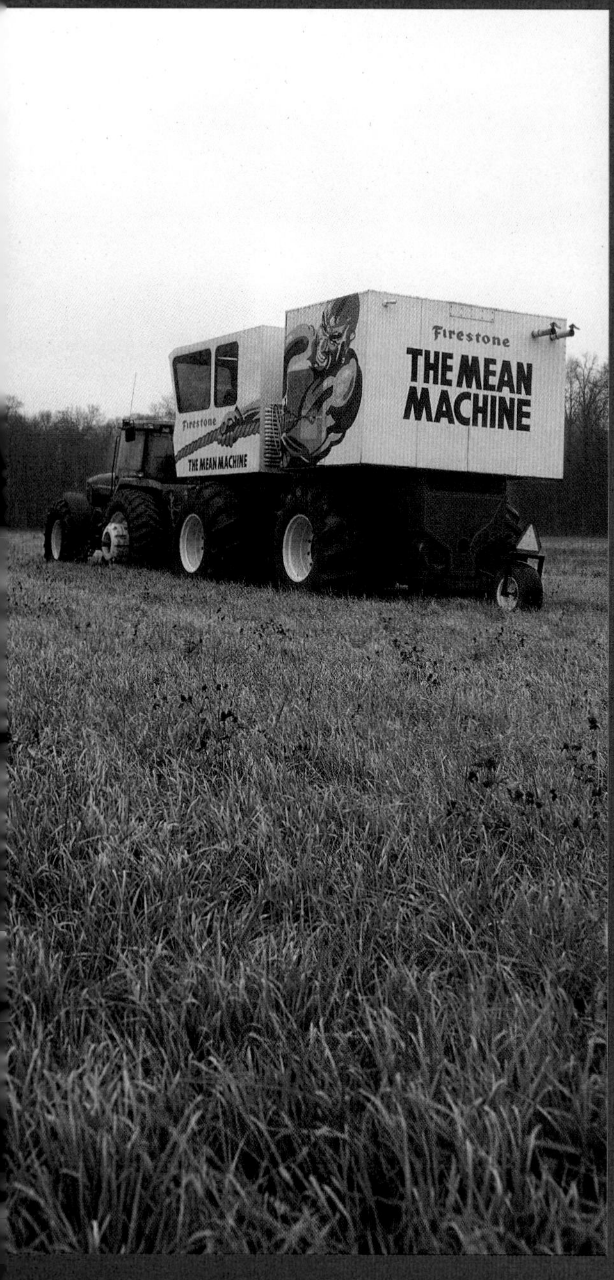

A "Firestone" still works the fields in founder Harvey S. Firestone's boyhood home of Columbiana, Ohio, except today, it's the Firestone Mean Machine that puts prototype Firestone agriculture tires through their paces at the company's test facility.
(Bridgestone/Firestone Collection)

From the beginning, Harvey S. Firestone made it his personal as well as corporate crusade to help the farmer. The steel wheels of the early tractor were terrible instruments of torture for most farmers. Their hard ride and relentless vibration left the driver worn out and battered after a day's work. Steel wheels also slipped and provided little traction. Seeing the great need for bringing rubber to the rural landscape, Firestone returned again and again to the family farm in Columbiana, where he experimented with rubber farm tires. Once perfected, he popularized his new rubber tractor tires with plowing contests. As word of these tests spread, the enthusiasm of bone-weary farmers was overwhelming.

"Development of a satisfactory farm tire was announced in 1931," recorded the Firestone book, *Pioneer and Pacemaker,* published for the company's 50th anniversary. "The increased economy, traction and comfort provided by these tires were so convincing that farmers rapidly changed from steel wheels to rubber-tired wheels."

Today more than 1,200 Firestone farm tire dealers provide expertise, top quality tires, and in-field service to farmers around the world.

In Columbiana, where Harvey S. Firestone learned firsthand about the farm, the company still maintains its primary testing facility for farm tires.

Emergency Fires Creativity

Throughout its hundred-year history, Firestone has responded to the call of freedom with the same determination and innovative spirit that powered its products.

The company was only in its teenage years when World War I broke out in 1914. But it had a work force of 10,500 men that was made available, if needed, for the war effort. Its newest plant was converted immediately to manufacture Army observation balloons, parts for gas masks, and millions of rubber tires, tubes, and steel tires for artillery wheels. During the first war to end all wars, 2,086 Firestone employees served with the Armed Forces.

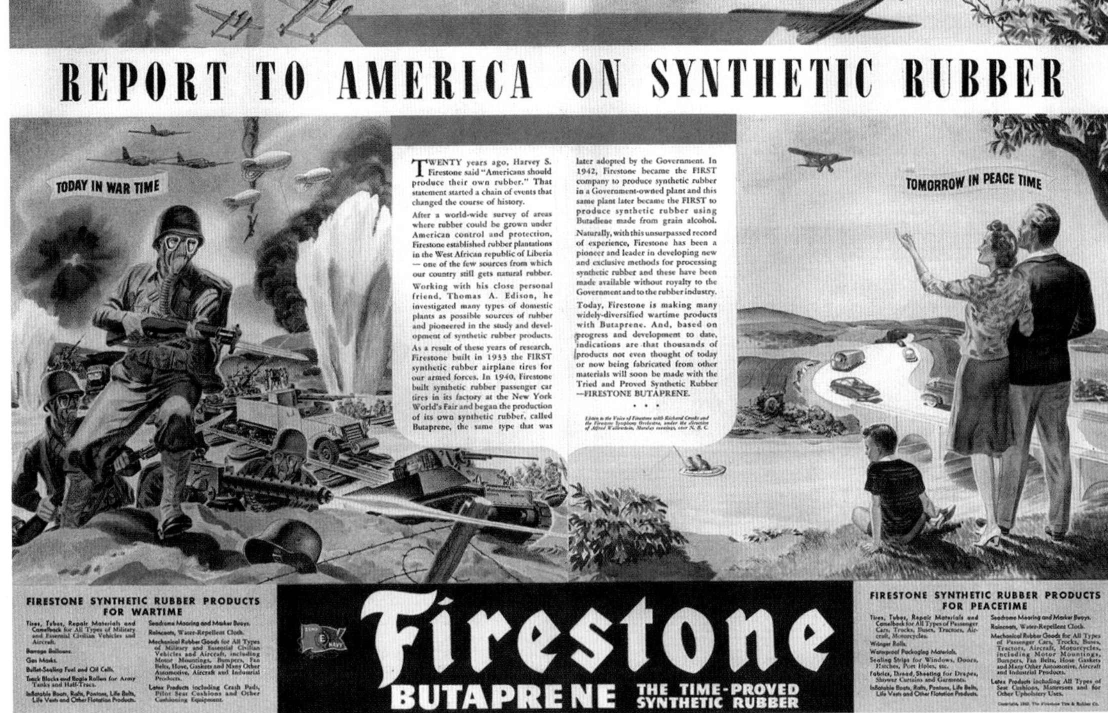

In a 1943 ad, Firestone heralds its accomplishments in the development and production of synthetic rubber for both war and peace-time uses. In the year prior to this ad, the company became the first to produce synthetic rubber in a government-owned plant.
(Bridgestone/Firestone Collection)

"A great emergency seems to fire the imagination of men and enable them to accomplish tasks which in ordinary times would appear utterly impossible," said Harvey S. Firestone.

By the time World War II broke out, a more mature company—one tested by both the First World War and the Great Depression—was poised to face a far greater challenge. In 1941, Firestone was one of America's premier manufacturers and was acutely aware of the importance of large-scale, high-production industries in a time of global crisis.

Rubber Plants and Victory Gardens

The company approached World War II with the same "can do" attitude it had enlisted in World War I. It gave every encouragement possible to employees entering the Armed Service. Out of the 10,000 employees subject to the draft, Firestone asked the government for only nine exemptions. Everyone who was

Firestone produced barrage balloons during World War II to protect troops from enemy aircraft. (As with most factories at that time, female workers "manned" many Firestone facilities during the war.)
(Modern Tire Dealer Archives)

During the First World War, Firestone workers tread the cobblestone streets of Akron, encouraging efforts to produce home-grown foods to free up food supplies for the troops. (Company employees would again take to their yards during World War II to grow these Victory Gardens.)

(University of Akron Archives – Firestone Collection)

purchasing Firestone stock or homes in Firestone Park was permitted to suspend payments while in the service without affecting their equity. To keep them in touch with the home front, Firestone mailed copies of all its employee publications to soldiers and sailors around the world.

The employees who remained at home during World War II exceeded their Liberty Bond quotas by raising almost $3.8 million. When President Roosevelt called on citizens to donate scrap rubber to the war effort, Firestone employees did their part, contributing old tires, water bottles, shoe heels, tennis balls, sink drain pads, fly swatters, and teething rings.

Firestone also encouraged employees on the home front to plant "Victory Gardens" by offering plots to employees. Homegrown vegetables helped the war effort by increasing the farm-raised produce sent to the troops. The company even went so far as to supply each gardener with one pound of insecticide to control the "ceaseless problem" of insects.

At the same time, Harvey S. Firestone, Jr., served on the Ohio Council of Defense and sponsored the creation of the Rubber Division which led to reductions in production and distribution costs of rubber products.

A Rubber Arsenal to be Reckoned With

Before it was over, the company found itself deeply involved in every aspect of the war effort. With its work force stretched to the limit, much of the new work was assigned to non-traditional plant workers—women.

"War changes everything, especially in a factory town," observed the Akron *Beacon Journal.* Women at Firestone and other Akron rubber companies during World War II found themselves called upon to do the work left by the men who had gone to battle.

Harvey S. Firestone, Jr., informed the government that the company wanted to do something challenging to aid the war effort. So in February 1941, when asked what he thought about manufacturing certain weapon parts and assembling them to make 40-millimeter anti-aircraft guns called Bofors, Harvey Firestone,

More than 25,000 employees of The Firestone Tire & Rubber Company gather at Firestone Stadium in August of 1942 to receive the Army-Navy Production Award – the E for efficiency.

(University of Akron Archives – Firestone Collection)

Just Imagine

A bank established by the founding family, subsidized housing created by Harvey S. Firestone, rent-free garden lots, and free life insurance—employees of The Firestone Tire & Rubber Company in those early years enjoyed a far-reaching relationship with the company. It reflected the paternalistic and altruistic character of the age. Imagine a company-maintained clubhouse for employees, complete with its own clubhouse band to play at company dances. Now, add a Glee Club, Male Chorus, Jazz Orchestra, and Symphony. Imagine too, a company baseball team good enough to play exhibition games against Major League teams and to enjoy its own spring training. Also include all sorts of sports opportunities: intramural baseball leagues (four of them), softball, soccer, tennis, bowling, and just about any other sport whether major or minor—everything from checkers tournaments to roller polo, indoor baseball, and boxing. Throw in cabarets, educational courses, and parties galore like a Christmas party for 12,000 kids and their parents, complete with first-run movies and live circus acts. Now top it all off with a pioneering stock-ownership plan.

Under the stewardship of Harvey S. Firestone, all of this and more was available from The Firestone Tire & Rubber Company.

Of all the recreational activities offered to employees by The Firestone Tire & Rubber Company, bowling was always the most popular. In this 1966 photograph, Akron's Dick Hoover, one of the nation's top professional bowlers, shows Mario A. DiFederico, president of the Firestone International Company, the proper grip. (University of Akron Archives – Firestone Collection)

Jr., answered without hesitation, "We're eager and willing." Even though it had never made weapons before, Firestone would quickly prove its ability. By March 31, 1944, it produced 25,000 of the Swedish-designed guns used extensively in the war. Women performed much of the production work.

Quality, not just quantity, had always been important to the company, so Firestone simplified the gun's design and reduced the number of parts it required. In the process, it built a better gun.

In 1958, Firestone President Raymond C. Firestone inspects the first working model of a new system designed and built for launching the U.S. Navy's Regulus guided missile from the deck of a submarine. The launch mechanisms were only one part of the arsenal of military products produced by Firestone.
(Cleveland Public Library)

From aircraft wings to rocket launchers, Firestone began crafting a growing arsenal of military equipment while still managing to produce a record number of tires for military vehicles. The company that offered one-stop shopping to the general public provided nearly the same service to the government. Increasingly the call was for aircraft tires. The industry as a whole increased its production of aircraft tires from 625,000 in 1942 to 1.4 million by 1944.

Probably the biggest contribution the company made to the war effort, however, was joining the challenge to create a synthetic substitute for natural rubber. Raymond F. Dunbrook, a principal member of Firestone's team, went to Washington, D.C., in 1944 to serve as chief of the War Production Board's polymer research branch. The challenge was met successfully and synthetic rubber factories sprung up all over the country.

Large military vehicles maneuvered the terrain of Vietnam on 36-ply tires crafted by Firestone. The tires stood more than nine-feet high and were mounted on wheels turned by individual motors.
(University of Akron Archives – Firestone Collection)

Cold War Heats Up Innovation

The uneasy peace that greeted the end of World War II seemed more like a time to mobilize for the next conflict. The next conflict wasn't long in coming. At the time the Korean conflict began in 1950, Firestone was already deeply involved in making military materials, producing rockets, recoilless rifles, anti-aircraft guns, 90-mm tank guns, and ammunition.

Of all the defense products Firestone supplied, the largest category in terms of dollars was tires. Tracks and other tank components came next. Fuel cells for ground vehicles and airplanes followed. Other war-effort products included floats, rubber boats, life vests, pneumatic dunnage bags, and huge collapsible fuel storage tanks.

During the Vietnam War, Firestone was providing a new generation of innovative products. Among the most interesting was a prefabricated rubber surfacing material that could be deployed quickly as aircraft landing strips in the jungle.

In 1951, in the dense Cold War fog that shrouded the project in secrecy for two years, Firestone began work on the first surface-to-surface ballistic guided missile—the Corporal. While it was never fired in anger, the new missile performed the powerful Cold War task of deterring would-be enemies of the United States.

As President Eisenhower himself marveled, "Four battalions of Corporal missiles are equivalent in firepower to all the artillery used in World War II on all fronts."

Firestone's involvement began as a production-only role. The company assembled and organized the entire system at a former tire plant managed by Leonard K. Firestone, one of the founder's sons and president of the company's California subsidiary. It was an awesome task since the missile system was built with 2,000 parts, seven miles of wire, radar control, launching systems, and "the brain power and mechanical skill of thousands."

Before its debut as a missile builder was complete, Firestone was named the contractor for all ancillary equipment for launching the missile as well as supervising its engineering and redesign.

The Corporal was conceived as a weapon to support ground combat operations. It was able to deliver a warhead—either conventional or nuclear—at supersonic speed in any weather to an exact target. It stood 46 feet tall and about 30 inches in diameter. Its exact range was never publicly released, but was certainly greater than 75 miles.

It was the first American ballistic artillery weapon and the Army's only missile in operational use. And it was from Firestone.

Harvey Firestone, Jr., Chairman, and Leonard K. Firestone, President of the Firestone Tire & Rubber Company of California, are pictured in 1954 inspecting the design and construction of a Corporal guided missile, manufactured by Firestone in Los Angeles. The company was a pioneer in warhead-carrying weapons which traveled at several times the speed of sound.
(Cleveland Public Library)

A Good Turn

Even among a family known for its generosity, Raymond Firestone's giving spirit was legendary.

One of the sons of the company's founder, he "made perhaps the largest impact of any individual from the rubber families," reported the Akron *Beacon Journal.*

Throughout his life, he made gifts to the Akron City Hospital and lent his support to Pegasus Farm in Hartville, Ohio, which runs an equestrian facility for physically challenged children. He contributed a Firestone room to the John S. Knight Center in Akron and sold his Bath Township estate to Ohio State University for $5 million (at least $3 million below its market value). When he died in 1994, Raymond Firestone left $2 million to his alma mater, Princeton University, but he also left $1 million to the University of Akron's School of Polymer Engineering. He left another $1 million to Akron City Hospital, part of Summa Health Systems, as well as $1 million to the Cleveland Clinic.

Raymond C. Firestone, the Chief Executive Officer and Chairman of the Executive Committee of The Firestone Tire & Rubber Company, shown here in 1976.

(American Highway Users Alliance Archives)

Some other significant Firestone contributions include:

- The donation of the family's West Akron polo fields as a site for St. Paul's Episcopal Church on West Market Street, earning it the nickname "St. Harvey's of the Polo Field." Over the years, the family provided considerable financial support to the church, including a charitable trust. The chapel there is named in honor of Harvey Firestone, Sr.'s wife, Idabelle.
- Endowment of the Firestone Conservatory of Music at the University of Akron and the former Idabelle Firestone School of Nursing at Akron City Hospital.
- The donation of more than $1 million in the '40s to build a library at Princeton, the alma mater of all five of Harvey S. Firestone's sons. Individual and family grants have continued to support the expansion of the Harvey S. Firestone Memorial Library.

The Firestone family's heritage of charitable giving continues through the Bridgestone/Firestone Trust Fund. The Firestone Tire & Rubber Company established the fund in 1952 with a donation of $1 million. It took its current name when Bridgestone and Firestone merged in 1990. The fund, which has grown considerably in market value over the years, makes donations each year to nonprofit organizations in four major categories—education; civic and community; culture and the arts; and health and welfare. The funded organizations are located primarily in communities where the company maintains plants and offices.

In 1998, the company made another generous contribution to society—this time the gift was a parcel of land. Bridgestone/Firestone donated approximately four thousand acres of wilderness to the people and State of Tennessee. Known as the Bridgestone/Firestone Conservation Area, the spectacular property is situated on Tennessee's Cumberland Plateau and is home to a number of rare and endangered species of animals and wildflowers. Special restrictions on the site guarantee that generations to come will enjoy the land's natural beauty and wonder.

The 4,000 acres of wilderness land given to the State of Tennessee by Bridgestone/Firestone stretches along Tennessee's spectacular Cumberland Plateau.
(Bridgestone/Firestone Collection)

WESTERN UNION
NEWCOMB CARLTON, PRESIDENT
J. C. WILLEVER, FIRST VICE
MR. H. S. FIRESTONE
% FIRESTONE TIRE & RUBBER COMPANY
PORTLAND OREGON
MAY 3
DRIVING MY TYDOL SPECIAL EQUIPPED WITH FIRESTONE HIGH
TIRES I WON THE INDIANAPOLIS FIVE HUNDRED MILE RACE TOD
THE SECOND TIME HAVING PREVIOUSLY WON IT IN 1928 STOP TH
THAT I HAD NO TIRE TROUBLE ENABLED ME TO SET A NEW SPEED
OF 104.162 MILES PER HOUR STOP I WANT TO CONGRATULATE YOU A
EXPRESS MY APPRECIATION FOR BUILDING TIRES THAT STAND UP UN
THE TERRIBLE PUNISHMENT WE MUST GIVE THEM IN RACING AND CARRI
ME SAFELY TO VICTORY
LOUIS MEYER
Firestone
DE LUXE CHAMPION
50
Belond
EXHAUST SPECIAL
PATRICK
Firestone
CHAMPION
THE TIRE WITH THE NEW SAFETY-LOCK
ORD BODY AND THE NEW GEAR-GRIP TREAD
The Only Tires Made That Are
Safety-Proved On The Speedway
For Your Protection On The Highway

CHAPTER 6

WIN ON SUNDAY, SELL ON MONDAY

6

Racing sales, the 47-year reign, and Firestone's legendary return to the racetrack

It's no accident that many of the great technological innovations of the 20th century have revolved around speed—from rocket ships to microchips, the cellular phone to fax machine. So it's quite natural that our highest-ranking professional spectator sport is auto racing. No other sport so accurately reflects the sensibilities of a society with an insatiable need for speed.

"CHOICE OF EUROPE AND AMERICA"
JULES GOUX IN HIS FRENCH PEUGEOT WHO DROVE TO VICTORY ON Firestone STOCK TIRES
SPENCER WISHART IN HIS AMERICAN-MADE MERCER WHO WON SECOND PLACE ON Firestones

An early Firestone ad is inscribed with personal notes of appreciation to the company from winning driver Jules Goux and runner-up Spencer Wishart.
(Bridgestone/Firestone Collection)

So we are drawn to the racetrack, to experience life in the fast lane, to see the split-second decisions that spell the difference between winning and losing.

From the very beginning, Harvey S. Firestone understood the power of the racetrack to drive product in the marketplace. This strategy continues to power the company's advertising.
(Bridgestone/Firestone Collection)

Selling Life Insurance

According to a 1925 Firestone publication, auto racing was "an unexcelled testing ground where months of ordinary wear are crowded into a few hours." In addition, the track, unlike traditional testing grounds, was open to the public—a distinct advantage for a company wishing to showcase its newest products. The track drew attention to the most marketable characteristics of tires—consistency, durability, and reliability. It proved a wonderful path for generating immediate product awareness and allowed racecar drivers to speak for the quality of the brand.

After all, a driver's life and livelihood depend on the car and tires.

From the very start of motorsports, a racecar driver's word on a product was gospel to the consumer. If a driver casually commented on the reliability and safety of his tires, sales would soar. Or, as Firestone liked to put it—"Win on Sunday, Sell on Monday."

The potential benefits of an association with racecar drivers was underscored first for Firestone in 1909. After completing a 60-mile-per-hour test at Indianapolis, the legendary daredevil and dirt-track driver Barney Oldfield

FIREHAWK
AFTER PERFORMING AT 172 MPH IN THE RAIN,
55 MPH IS A PIECE OF CAKE.
INDY PERFORMANCE. FOR THE RAIN. FOR THE ROAD. Firehawk SZ50® ultra-high performance tire. With a tire tread patterned after our original Firehawk Indy* racing rain tire, the Firehawk SZ50 is well equipped to handle a wide range of conditions from heat-baked highways to rain-drenched curves.
FOR THE RAIN. The Firehawk SZ50 derives its Power-V® tread from our original Firehawk Indy* racing rain tire. This unique tread pattern channels water out of the tire's path. It's so effective, it gives Indy* drivers the confidence they need to scream into wet turns. It's a difference you can actually feel in your own driving.
FOR THE ROAD. The Firehawk SZ50 delivers all the performance characteristics you'd expect from an ultra-high performance tire. The feel of the road. The tight handling. The precise cornering. And one more. It's exceptionally quiet.
COOL PERFORMANCE. You might not know it, but temperature has a lot to do with a tire's performance. Most traditional high-performance tires perform better in high temperature ranges. But the Firehawk SZ50 maintains exceptional performance when it's hot and when it's cool.
HIGH-PERFORMANCE CARS DESERVE HIGH-PERFORMANCE TIRES. Get the performance you paid for when you bought your high-performance car. Performance technology that comes from the tires of the highest-performing cars in America. The Indy* cars. And the ultra-high performance that the Firehawk SZ50 can deliver. So, ask your Firestone retailer about the Firehawk SZ50. And find out what Indy* proven technology can do for your high-performance car.
FIREHAWK SZ50
For the Rain. For the Road.
Firehawk Indy* Racing Rain Tire
Firehawk SZ50
uni-T
Ultimate Tire Technology
UNI-T Is The Difference
UNI-T, the Ultimate Network of Intelligent Tire Technology, is a total rethinking of the automobile tire combining three principle technologies.
CO-CS® Innovative Tire Design
• A Comprehensive Tire Design Method
O-Bead® Innovative Roundness
• Rounder Is Better
L.L. Carbon® Innovative New Compound
• Longer Is Stronger
Firestone
STOCK TIRES
FIRST & SECOND
America's Tire Since 1900
1-800-807-9555
www.firestone-usa.com
* Indy® is a registered trademark of the Indianapolis Motor Speedway.

Barney Oldfield, one of the earliest American racecar drivers, fondly referred to his Firestone Tires as his "only life insurance."
(Bridgestone/Firestone Collection)

stepped from his car and casually commented, "My only life insurance is my Firestone tires."

With this bold, straightforward utterance, Firestone became a motorsports marketing pioneer. Years later, C. B. Ryan, director of advertising for Firestone, said the Oldfield comment was one of the first advertising benefits ever tied to a sport.

Oldfield went on to win that Indianapolis race in 1909. It was the first Indianapolis 300, a precursor to the Indy 500® that would figure so prominently in Firestone's race through the 20th century.

Eventually Oldfield became part of the Firestone team and barnstormed race tracks across the country in a car sporting a big banner emblazoned with his famous line—"My only life insurance is my Firestone tires."

"This is an age of speed. Modern man demands more speed and then still more speed. The geniuses of the automobile world vie with one another to produce marvelous pieces of mechanism that will travel still faster with comparative safety."

– Harvey S. Firestone, 1931

Birth of a Brickyard Tradition

Because of the quality and performance of its products, Firestone was beginning to attract drivers. It still lacked a major platform from which to tout its racing accomplishments. So in 1911, when the company's Indianapolis branch manager proposed Firestone back a driver in the new 500-mile "Sweepstakes" race to be run on Decoration Day (the forerunner of Memorial

FIRESTONE WINS

AT INDIANAPOLIS 500...42nd CONSECUTIVE VICTORY

First 7 places on Firestone—only 2 cars on competitive tires able to finish race.

JIM CLARK
1965 winner at 150.686 mph.

"I ran on Firestone tires because I knew I could count on them. They did a wonderful job!"

Once again, the winning car at the famous Indianapolis 500 raced on Firestone tires to prove—if more proof were needed—that Firestone is still the greatest tire name in racing. This year's win marks Firestone's 42nd consecutive victory in the 500—a remarkable unbroken streak that dates back to 1920. For over 50 years, in fact, the Firestone name has been synonymous with racing research. In that time more races have been won on Firestone tires than any others.

But it's not what we get out of winning—it's what *you* get. Out of our leadership in building tires for race cars comes an unequalled experience in building tires for your car—tires that are safer, stronger and last much longer. Tires with the same Sup-R-Tuf rubber and tough Super-Weld body construction that we put into our race tires, tires we back confidently with a nationwide guarantee.

Next time you need tires, get the ones that are speedway-proved for your highway safety. Firestone tires. You can charge them, if you like, at your nearby Firestone Dealer or Store.

Sup-R-Tuf®, Super-Weld—Firestone T.M.

No races during the war years.

Firestone

THE GREATEST TIRE NAME IN RACING FOR OVER 50 YEARS

Driver Jim Clark keeps Firestone's legendary Indianapolis 500 winning streak rolling with Firestone's 42nd consecutive victory at Indy. The victorious Clark said simply, "I ran on Firestone tires because I knew I could count on them. They did a wonderful job!"

(Bridgestone/Firestone Collection)

Day), Firestone was quick to see the possibilities. The enterprising branch manager also suggested that if the Firestone driver won the first Indy 500, the company might wish to spend $50,000 advertising the fact. Harvey S. Firestone thought it was a fantastic idea. A tradition was born.

From its earliest days, winning the Indy 500 had a lot to do with the number of pitstops a driver made. Each stop reduced a car's overall average speed. So if a set of tires lasted as long as a tank of gasoline, the number of stops was reduced and the chances of winning improved dramatically. That's precisely where consistency, durability, and reliability came in. Firestone tire designers worked to ensure their tires survived the race even under the harshest track conditions. Over the years, this priority of product quality has paid off.

When Ray Harroun won the inaugural 500-mile race in 1911, three tires never had to be changed. The fourth, the right rear tire, which took the most punishment on the turns, was changed only three times—once as a precaution. Other cars made as many as 15 tire changes.

From that winning moment, Harvey S. Firestone was sold on making the great two-and-one-half mile racing oval in Indianapolis his prime speed and endurance proving ground. Following the recommendation of his Indianapolis branch manager, he advertised each win.

After his victory, Harroun retired from racing. Firestone had no driver in 1912, and there wouldn't have been one in 1913 if it wasn't for a French driver named Jules Goux, driving a Peugeot, who was frustrated that his French-made tires split in two during the race's trial runs. Goux, eager to win at Indianapolis, accepted an invitation to run on Firestone tires and went on to win the race.

'Firestone Makes No Racing Tires'

Firestone owned the rest of 1913. At every major race for the rest of the year, Firestone tires were on the winning car. The ads surrounding these wins were classic.

"Firestone makes no racing tires," the ads proclaimed, adding, "Every event is being won on the regular tires that any motorist gets when he buys Firestone."

The association with racing drove its tires out of the stores—profits rose to $1.6 million and Firestone's common stock sold as high as $360 a share before the year was out. Firestone dealers were deeply aware of what racing victories and land speed records claimed by Firestone tires meant to their sales.

From 1913, Firestone was everywhere there was racing—Pike's Peak hill-climbing races, endurance races on public roads like those from New York to San Francisco and Toledo to Montreal, Grand Prix events, and local dirt track

Who better than Ab Jenkins, the World's Safest Driver, to tout the safety of Firestone's triple-safe tires in this 1937 ad? (Bridgestone/Firestone Collection)

Hometown favorite driver Wilbur Shaw rode Firestone tires to victory at the Indianapolis 500 in 1937, 1939 and 1940. He came close to the top spot on three other occasions, finishing second in 1933, 1935 and 1938. (University of Akron Archives – Firestone Collection)

races throughout the country—but atop all else was the Indianapolis 500.

Year after year, Firestone dealers, company executives, and employees basked in the reflected glory as the winners at Indianapolis broke speed and endurance records on Firestone tires. From 1920 through 1966, Firestone tires set every Indy 500 record imaginable. In fact, during that remarkable 47-year period, it failed to do just one thing—lose a race!

It was a winning tradition unmatched in motorsports.

Because of his leadership, Harvey S. Firestone was recognized as one of the pioneer patrons of Indy car racing. In honor of that, the race's governing body named him referee of the 1929 Indianapolis Sweepstakes, as the Indy 500 was called during its early days. In 1930, the Race Drivers Association presented Firestone with a medal, inscribed "In appreciation of his untiring cooperation and leadership in the consistent development of tires which have contributed to the establishment of automobile safety and endurance records."

Perhaps the highest honor bestowed on Firestone came posthumously in 1974 when he was inducted into the newly organized Automobile Racing Hall of Fame as one of 10 racing pioneers.

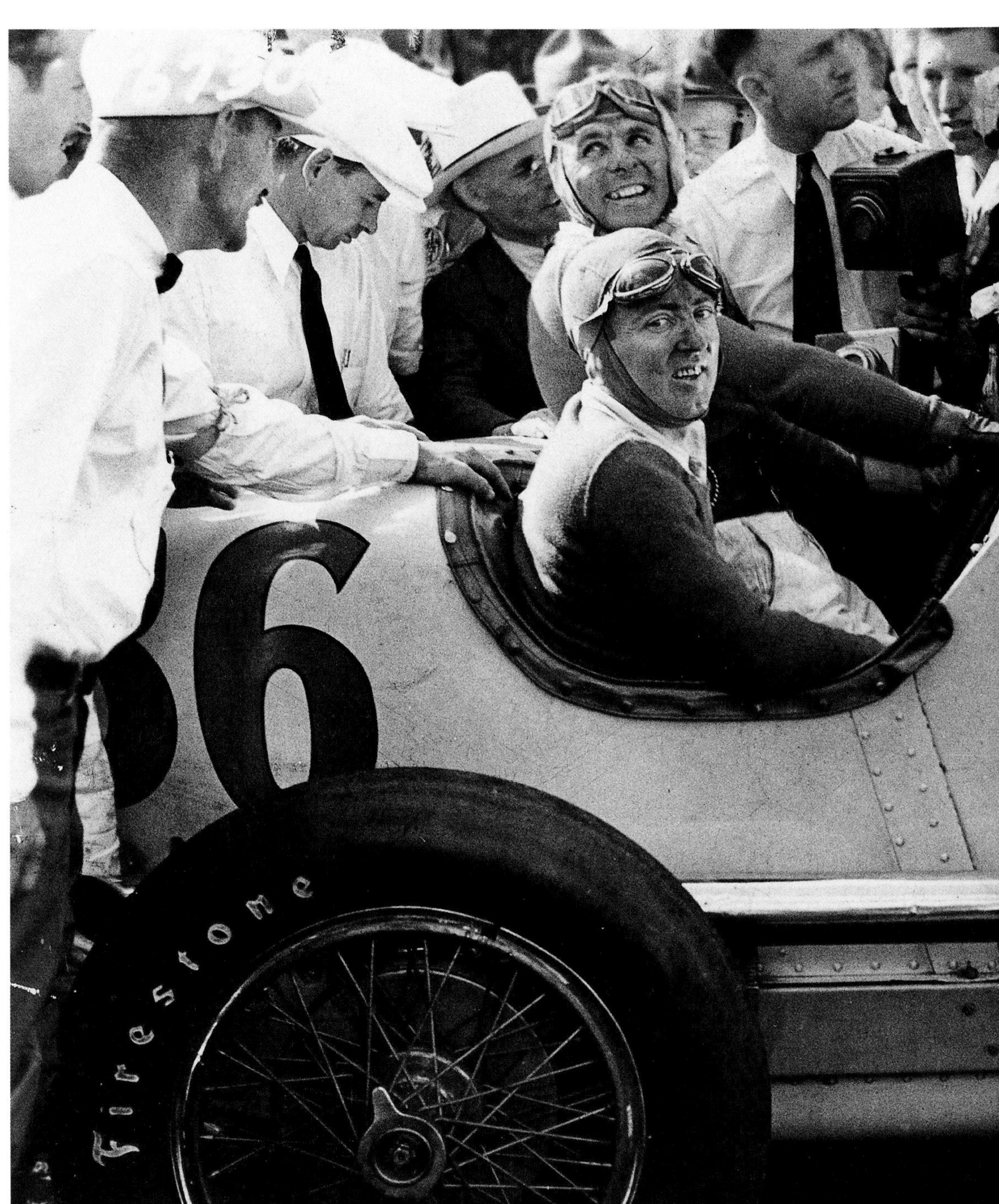

Louis Meyer, the first three-time winner of the Indianapolis 500, raced to his record-setting performances aboard Firestone tires. Roaring to victory lane in 1928, 1933 and 1936, Meyer established speed records in his last two wins and recorded his first victory at the age of 23.

(Bridgestone/Firestone Collection)

The value of the track as a test site was proven again and again as pioneering advances in the basic components and materials of a car, particularly tires, were rolled out at Indy. Among the Firestone innovations to win at Indy were non-skid treads, low-pressure balloon tires, and gum-dipping to insulate tire cords against internal heat, and nylon cords.

"The racing program shortens the time needed for getting a tire from concept to market to under a year," said Dick Davis, general manager of Firestone racing. Testing under racing conditions allows engineers to extrapolate wear on the streets.

Rookie British driver Graham Hill, fresh from his 1966 Indianapolis win, pauses from his celebration to report, "Firestone tires gave me championship performance and safety in winning this 500-mile race." (University of Akron Archives – Firestone Collection)

On a Winning Route in '66

Through the first half-century of its history, racing was the centerpiece of Firestone marketing. In 1966, a Firestone report on racing activities highlighted the company's major accomplishments for the year, including the following:

- Jimmy Clark of Scotland won the U.S. Grand Prix at Watkins Glen on Firestone tires, the first time a winner of this grueling test of endurance ran on American-made tires.
- Jackie Stewart, another Scot, was voted "Rookie of the Year" at Indianapolis and won the first 200-mile race for Indy cars at Mt. Fuji, Japan, International Speedway.
- Italian-born Mario Andretti of Nazareth, Pennsylvania, won the United States Auto Club (USAC) driving championship for the second year in a row after a host of wins using Firestone tires.
- James Hall and James R. "Hap" Sharp, two American inventors and drivers from Midland, Texas, incorporated many of their own innovations into their Firestone-shod Chaparral sports cars, and won major events including races at Riverdale, Nassau, Laguna Seca, and Nurburgring.

Firestone experienced wins in a variety of racing series' venues, including drag racing, with this 1973 Sox & Martin drag car.
(Bridgestone/Firestone Collection)

- Graham Hill became the oldest rookie ever to win at Indy and continued Firestone's winning tradition at the Brickyard with its 43rd consecutive victory in the race's Golden Anniversary. In an exciting race, Hill fended off the challenge of two great Grand Prix drivers, Jackie Stewart and Jimmy Clark.

At the close of the 1966 racing season, Firestone had equipped winning cars in more places around the world than ever before.

With the 1967 season, however, Firestone witnessed the end of auto racing's most enduring and remarkable streak. Racing a unique turbine-powered car equipped with Firestone tires, Parnelli Jones came within 10 miles of victory at Indy. Though it was close, there was no trip to the Brickyard's victory circle.

Firestone's Indy winning streak finally came to a close, but not for long.

The company came back to win in 1969 with Mario Andretti, and again in 1970 and 1971 with back-to-back wins by Al Unser.

In 1972, three major auto racing championships were won with Firestone tires. The tires carried Emerson Fittipaldi of Brazil to the World Driving Championship, propelled the Ferrari racing team to top honors in the World Manufacturer's Championship, and won the United States Auto Club championship division title for the second consecutive year with driver Joe Leonard.

Firestone Takes a Pit Stop

In 1974, Firestone shocked the racing world when it made the decision to leave motorsports.

"Firestone, one of the more familiar names in big-time auto racing, has black-flagged its major racing program and pulled out of the Indy 500 and other major U.S. Auto Club and

Raymond C. Firestone congratulates 1950 Indy 500 winner, Johnny Parsons, on setting a new Indianapolis 500 record of 124.002 miles per hour.
(University of Akron Archives — Firestone Collection)

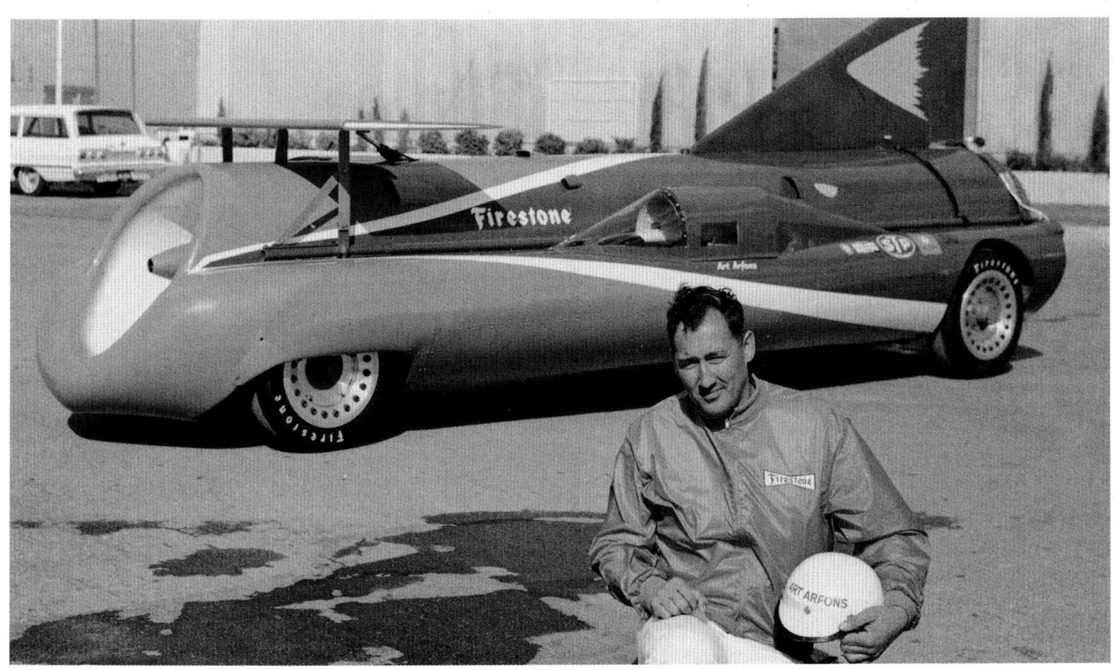

Firing mankind's passion for greater and greater speed, Firestone tires were part of the advanced equipment team that propelled driver Art Arfons and his Green Monster to a land speed record in 1964.
(Bridgestone/Firestone Collection)

Formula races," reported *Modern Tire Dealer* magazine when it ran the bad news in its September 1974 issue.

Firestone withdrew from racing in its 75th year as a company. Even so, Firestone's reputation continued to move tires. During the 1975–76 season, sales to the racing market reached a new high, a 10 percent increase over the previous year. Incredibly, three years later, Firestone performance tires were still showing improved sales.

With such a stunning record, why had Firestone taken itself out of the race? Budget and the popularity of radials played some part. The motorsports program was getting more and more expensive at a time when American consumers were increasingly choosing the new European radial tires for their passenger cars, rather than the bias plys that Firestone and other American tire manufacturers used on race cars. Left without Firestone as a challenger, a rival tire company was able to claim victories through the 1995 race.

The Legend Returns

Actually Firestone only took a hiatus from Indy car racing. For two decades. Then in 1993, as the new Bridgestone/Firestone Inc., it made a dramatic turnaround, after talking to dealers around the country. What dealers wanted was a return to Indy.

Al Speyer, director of Bridgestone/Firestone Motorsports; Yoichiro Kaizaki, Bridgestone/Firestone chairman and CEO; Shu Ishibashi, then director of Bridgestone/Firestone Consumer Tire Marketing and others traveled to Indianapolis in 1992. A visit to the track museum dramatized the long and rich history of the Firestone name at Indy.

Johnny Carson, longtime host of NBC's "Tonight Show," studies the 2 1/2-mile track at the Indianapolis Motor Speedway with 1963 Indy winner Parnelli Jones. Carson's 160 mph high-speed run around the Brickyard was telecast on his show September 29, 1967.
(University of Akron Archives – Firestone Collection)

FIRESTONE W

Record 50th Indy 500®

1911
Ray Harroun

1913
Jules Goux

1920
Gaston Chevrolet

1921
Tommy Milton

1922
Jimmy Murphy

1928
Louis Meyer

1929
Ray Keech

1930
Billy Arnold

1931
Louis Schneider

1932
Fred Frame

1938
Floyd Roberts

1939
Wilbur Shaw

1940
Wilbur Shaw

1941
M. Rose, F. Davis

1946
George Robson

1952
Troy Ruttman

1953
Bill Vukovich

1954
Bill Vukovich

1955
Bob Sweikert

1956
Pat Flaherty

1962
Rodger Ward

1963
Parnelli Jones

1964
A.J. Foyt

1965
Jim Clark

1966
Graham Hill

1997 Winner
Arie Luyendyk

S INDY AGAIN

ory For Firestone Tires

1923 Tommy Milton | 1924 L. Corum, Joe Boyer | 1925 Pete De Paolo | 1926 Frank Lockhart | 1927 George Souders

1933 Louis Meyer | 1934 Wild Bill Cummings | 1935 Kelly Petillo | 1936 Louis Meyer | 1937 Wilbur Shaw

1947 Mauri Rose | 1948 Mauri Rose | 1949 Bill Holland | 1950 Johnnie Parsons | 1951 Lee Wallard

1957 Sam Hanks | 1958 Jimmy Bryan | 1959 Rodger Ward | 1960 Jim Rathmann | 1961 A.J. Foyt

1969 Mario Andretti | 1970 Al Unser | 1971 Al Unser | 1996 Buddy Lazier

On May 27, 1997, Firestone challenged—and shattered—the ultimate Indy 500® record. Our own. Firestone Firehawk™ racing ires chalked up an astonishing 50th Indianapolis 500® win for the brand that has become an American Legend... rom Indy, to the interstates, to the street where you live.

Firestone returned to the Indy 500® because we knew the challenges of competition brings out the best, in our people and our tires. The same challenging spirit that leads us into the fiercely competitive world of Indy racing also drives our search or new consumer tire technologies. What we've learned along the way allows us to create an exciting new line-up of outstanding tires for your car.

We'd like to congratulate Arie Luyendyk on winning the 1997 Indy 500 on Firestone Firehawk racing tires, and salute all he teams and drivers that chose to compete on Firestone tires. And to everyone across America who chooses to drive on Firestone tires every day, thanks for being part of our winning tradition. Firestone. The Legend.

Race-Winning Firestone Firehawk™ Indy Racing Slick & Firestone Firehawk SS10™ Street Tire

Firestone Firehawk™ Indy Racing Rain Tire & Firestone Firehawk SZ50™ Ultra-High Performance Tire

Indy®, Indy 500® and Indianapolis 500® are registered trademarks of the Indianapolis Motor Speedway.

With Arie Luyendyk's 1997 Indy 500 win, Firestone reflects on its monumental Indy performances... an incredible journey that includes 50 trips to the winner's circle.

(Bridgestone/Firestone Collection)

Pausing in the pits at the 1995 Indianapolis 500, Scott Pruett was one of the world-class drivers who helped Firestone make its highly publicized return after two decades away from Indy car action.
(Bridgestone/Firestone Collection)

"Shu Ishibashi looked around and said simply, 'The Indy belongs to Firestone,' " remembered Speyer. The idea to return to racing was presented to Kaizaki and other top executives and approved.

"Nothing else could have returned value to the Firestone name in quite the same way," said Speyer.

For the first time in 20 years, the old rallying cry of "Win on Sunday, Sell on Monday" was uttered with a smile.

Firestone already had a bit of a head start on its heralded return to Indy. In 1991, the company began sponsoring Indy Lights, the developmental series for Indy car competition. The series provided a place for talented, young

With Scott Pruett at the wheel, Firestone returns to its winning ways at the 1995 Marlboro 500. In a dramatic run for the finish, Pruett just barely beats Al Unser Jr. to claim the checkered flag and the brand's first Indy car win since returning to the circuit after a 20-year absence.
(Bridgestone/Firestone Collection)

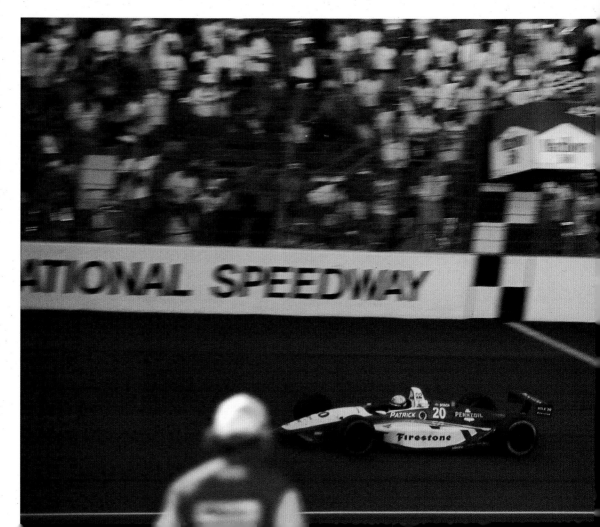

drivers to build experience before making the move up.

The company announced its return to Indy car racing in 1993 and used 1994 for extensive testing. Then, in 1995, Firestone was ready to return to the big one—the fabled Indy 500 at the Brickyard. The tire and motorsports worlds were buzzing over Firestone's return to the Memorial Day classic. Diehard racing fans, recalling the great Firestone wins, flooded Akron offices with telegrams, faxes, and e-mails. Employee enthusiasm more than reflected that of the fans and there was an immediate morale boost to the company's 33,450 U.S. employees and more than 12,000 retailers. The retailers stood ready to promote the line, looking for a rally in name recognition and prestige.

What they got was a renaissance.

"Firestone's return to racing had a significant impact on consumer confidence," said dealer Paul Bobzin of La Canada, California. "The ride quality and enhanced responsive handling characteristics of today's cars are a direct result of Firestone's return to racing.

"Consumers and employees want to be part of the racing scene."

Philadelphia dealer Charlie Thum agreed, "Our employees now feel like they're part of the [racing] team, and their enthusiasm spills over to our customers."

In 1998, Bridgestone/ Firestone moved its Indy Lights sponsorship from Firestone to Dayton tires in order to build the Dayton brand through trips to the winner's circle.
(Bridgestone/Firestone Collection)

Back Home Again in Indiana

It was like old times again when the Firestone name rolled back onto the Brickyard track at Indianapolis Motor Speedway. In its first Indy 500 race after the 20-year layoff—Memorial Day Weekend 1995—Firestone was making an excellent showing with two of its drivers leading the pack late in the race. It looked like Firestone might return right where it left off.

Firestone drivers Scott Goodyear and Scott Pruett were running 1 and 2 and nose to tail less than 20 laps from the finish. Then calamity struck. Pruett crashed and Scott Goodyear was penalized for passing the pace car under the yellow flag. The team that had come so far so fast, lost by so little. The team and crew were heartbroken.

Firestone's return to victory lane was only delayed. Later that year, in July, Scott Pruett won the Marlboro 500 race held at Michigan International Speedway.

"Nothing could resuscitate the Firestone name better and more effectively than a successful return to Indy racing," a company spokesperson was quoted in the *Wall Street Journal*.

Driver Buddy Lazier celebrates his 1996 Indy 500 win, and Firestone's first win since its return to the Brickyard.
(Bridgestone/Firestone Collection)

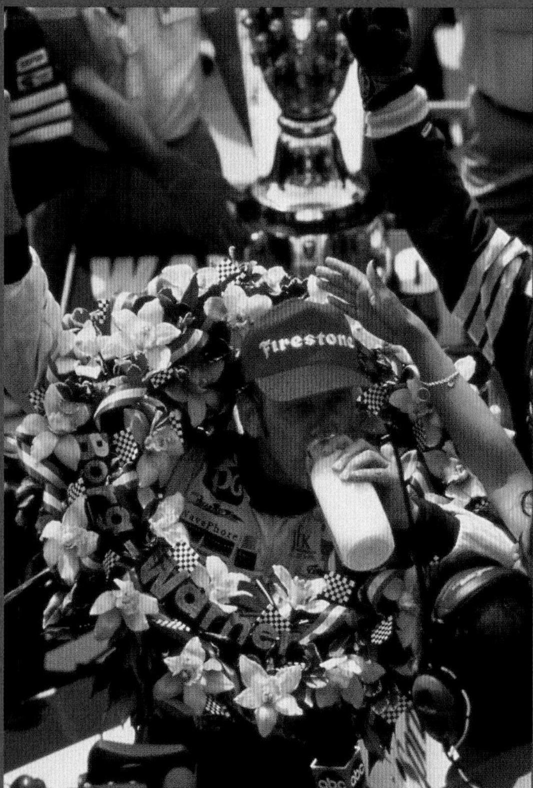

Arie Luyendyk enjoys the sweet taste of success downing the traditional quart of milk as the winner of the 1997 Indy 500. Luyendyk captures Firestone tires' historic 50th win – an unprecedented record in the annals of motorsports.
(Bridgestone/Firestone Collection)

Success came again one month later in the Loudon 200. The next year, in 1996, Firestone drivers posted six more wins at the Orlando 200, Homestead 200, Brazil 250, Phoenix 200, Australia 200, and the Long Beach 200. The seventh win of the season, however, was the sweetest of all.

On May 26, 1996, Buddy Lazier added his likeness to the Borg-Warner trophy. Driving a Reynard chassis powered with a Ford engine and riding on Firestone rubber, Lazier took the checkered flag at the Indianapolis 500. With six more wins before the year was out, Firestone was back in a big way.

Firestone had successfully completed the trip back to the place where it had proven itself and won for most of the century. With two-time Indy winner Arie Luyendyk's 1997 victory, Firestone earned its 50th Indy win, a record no other supplier—of tires, engines, or cars—has come close to touching.

A Driving Strategy for Success

In 1996, the Firestone racing program took part in 16 Championship Auto Racing Teams (CART) series races and drove away with 10 wins. The Indy Racing League (IRL) had five races that year and three of those events were won by drivers on Firestone tires. Overall, it won 13 of 21 races. The next year, it won 13 CART and six IRL—a total of 19 out of 25 races, or victories 76 percent of the time.

Meanwhile, the parent Bridgestone Corporation made the decision to enter Formula One racing to solidify its pinnacle position in motorsports technology. With early success (Bridgestone won Formula One in only its second year of participation) and partnering with top racing teams in 1998, Formula One was creating the same kind of impact for the Bridgestone brand as Indy car and Champ car racing were having for Firestone.

Zanardi driving in '98 Long Beach Grand Prix
(Bridgestone/Firestone Collection)

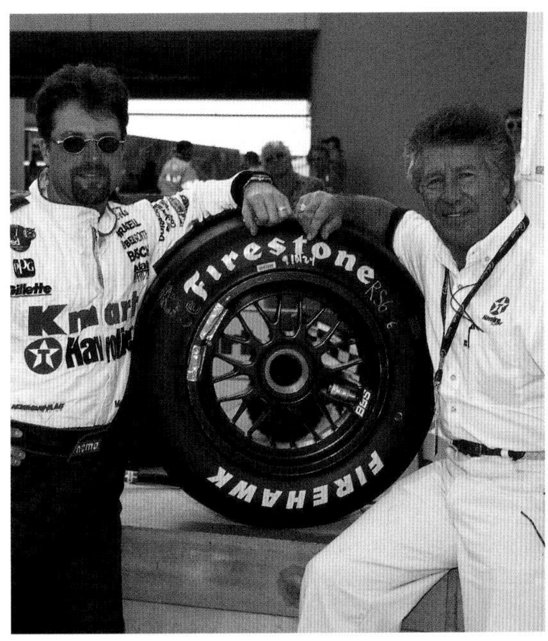

What's in a name? Just ask two of racing's legendary names – Michael and his father Mario Andretti about their Firestone tires. Mario won the 1969 Indy 500 on a single set of Firestone tires.
(Bridgestone/Firestone Collection)

Bridgestone/Firestone also decided to switch its Indy Lights sponsorship from Firestone to the Dayton brand for the 1998 season as part of an overall effort to raise that brand's market position. The Firestone Tire & Rubber Company had acquired Dayton Tire in 1961 and the line was now positioned to compete against Cooper, Uniroyal, and other value tire brands.

For Bridgestone/Firestone the entry into racing has served to strengthen its brands as a critical part of its global strategy.

Today, as it enters the 21st century, Firestone has taken the race to the next level. The race continues to drive the work of the company's Akron Technical Center, where it has rekindled the fire for invention, for newer and better tire technologies to test on the track on Sunday—ultimately, to win and sell its discoveries to the world come Monday.

Bridgestone Annual Report 1988

The Bridgestone-Firestone merger creates exciting opportunities for our companies to build on each other's immense capabilities in marketing, manufacturing, and product development.

Akira Yeiri
President,
Bridgestone Corporation

BRIDGE BS STONE

JOHN J. NEVIN
CHAIRMAN OF THE BOARD

ANNUAL REPORT OF THE FIRESTONE TIRE & RUBBER COMPANY

(FILE No. 275 OF 1934).

HASTINGS & CO.
Solicitors for the Applicants,
Gloucester Building, 2nd Floor,
Hong Kong.

CHAPTER 7

REINVENTING THE WHEEL

7

Radial changes, the world merges, and the 'stones' unite as Bridgestone/Firestone

Firestone has long enjoyed a rich history of bringing the world together— a world of people, industry, science, sport and culture.

Its tires and technology have helped traverse the distance between North and South, East and West, the country and the city. Its international operations brought economic stability, education, and technical know-how to far-flung manufacturing facilities, from

"Companies are just beginning to learn what nations have always known: in a complex, uncertain world filled with dangerous opponents, it is best not to go it alone. Great powers operating across broad theaters of engagement have traditionally made common cause with others whose interests ran parallel with their own. No shame in that. Entente—the striking of an alliance—is a responsible part of every good strategist's repertoire. In today's competitive environment, this is also true for corporate managers."

**– Kenichi Ohmae,
head of the Tokyo Office of McKinsey and Co., Harvard Business Review, March-April 1989**

Akron to Argentina, Africa to Australia. Its war efforts successfully brought the world together in a triumph over the conflicts that divided the globe. Its legendary work in racing united the best international talents with the best minds to put the company's work to the ultimate test. Its interest in culture and consumer transportation created quality programming to uplift a people and good roads to help erase the geographic divisions of a nation.

As it entered the 20th century's final few laps, The Firestone Tire & Rubber Company prepared to bring the world together once more in a milestone decision to merge with the Bridgestone Corporation in 1988.

It was a bold move that would reinvent the company as well as the tires that rolled off its assembly lines. In coming together, the two great entities navigated a difficult road, laden with international controversy, market intrigue, dramatic last-minute business heroics, and the monumental cooperation of two cultures. What has emerged from this melding of countries and cultures was well worth the journey.

Bridgestone received global recognition in 1968 when the company was awarded the internationally respected and coveted Deming Prize for excellence in quality.
(Bridgestone Corporation Archives)

Just as founder Harvey S. Firestone commanded the attention of presidents, here Bridgestone founder Shojiro Ishibashi demonstrates his company's advances in tire technology to Japanese Emperor Hirohito in 1949.
(Bridgestone Corporation Archives)

A Shared Quality

Despite being founded half a world apart, Bridgestone and Firestone shared a similar heritage. The resemblance stretched beyond sound-alike names. It arose from the heart and cultural core of both organizations. They shared a tradition of technical excellence that gave them their reputation for quality.

Harvey S. Firestone was a visionary leader who preached the virtue of quality over all other product identifiers and characteristics. He believed that the whole structure of business was making and doing useful things for others—things of quality.

On the other side of the world, Shojiro Ishibashi founded Bridgestone with a similar philosophy. His mantra was "serving society with products of superior quality." He was so successful in his pursuit that in 1968 his company won the coveted Deming Prize for quality. The award, named for Dr. W. Edwards Deming, recognizes corporations and individuals that demonstrate an outstanding commitment to quality and whose products or inventions make exceptional advances in the pursuit of quality. The award has been conferred on fewer than 100 companies since it was established in 1951.

The bedrock belief—that companies producing quality products and providing customer service always win out over those too willing to cut corners in the name of corporate efficiency—was a founding principle for both companies.

Although Firestone and Bridgestone shared business philosophies, it took business changes to prompt the two corporate giants to join forces.

Beginning with Bridgestone's original keystone logo in 1929 – strikingly similar to the original Firestone crest – the brand mark has undergone several updates to reflect the advancement of the company and its products.
(Bridgestone Corporation Archives)

From Tabis to Tires The Birth of Bridgestone

Besides similar sounding names, Bridgestone and Firestone share bold beginnings.

At the turn of the century, Harvey Firestone, Sr., abandoned the buggy business because of his belief in the future of the horseless carriage. Thirty years later in Japan, Shojiro Ishibashi, senior vice president of Nihon Tabi K.K., risked the future of an already successful business because of the potential he saw in making tires.

It was a bold step for a company already successful crafting rubber-soled traditional Japanese footwear—called zika tabis—as well as rubber-soled shoes similar to sneakers. Like Firestone, the company's success had been built on innovative marketing and technology. It was credited with establishing a single uniform price for tabis and developing a means for attaching rubber soles to footwear. Because of this success, Shojiro Ishibashi's brother and other trusted advisors argued against venturing into a business already dominated by American and British companies. Ishibashi, however, saw an opportunity in the 30 million yen tire market in Japan. He also saw an opportunity to serve his country.

"I intend to pursue this venture, not just for my family or for the sake of the company, but for the country," Ishibashi said.

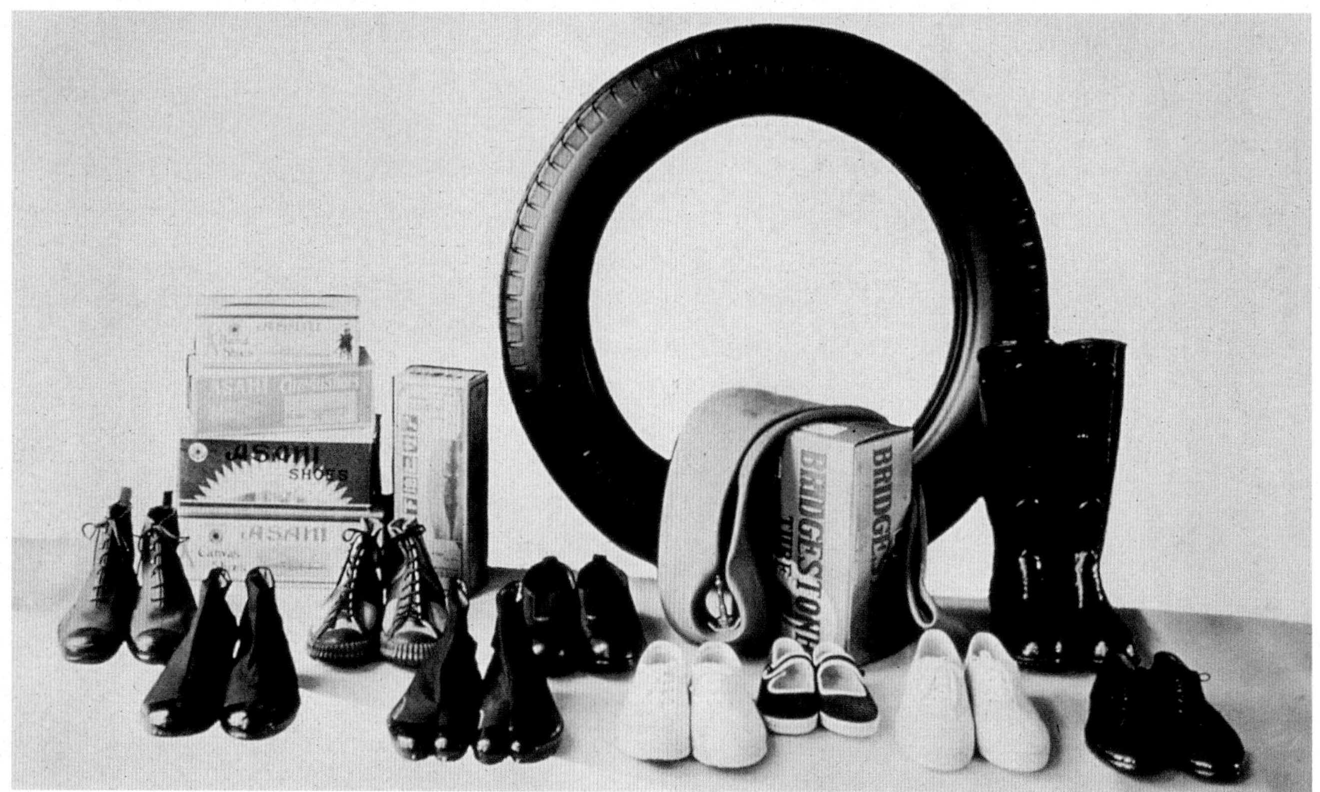

Paralleling Harvey S. Firestone's move from the horse and buggy business into tire manufacturing, by 1932 Nihon Tabi had made the leap from crafting shoes to pursuing the promise of tire manufacturing.
(Bridgestone Corporation Archives)

And so in 1929, ignoring the objections of advisors, Ishibashi secretly ordered tire-making machinery from the Standard Mold Company in Akron. That original order included two Banner tire-forming machines, a vacuum expander, five vertical vulcanizing machines, a compressor, vacuum pump, a rim press, and two tire molds. It was a modest start but it was enough equipment to craft 300 tires a day.

Workers at Bridgestone's first tire plant in Kurume, Japan, proudly pose in 1930 with early evidence of the company's craftsmanship. (Bridgestone Corporation Archives)

Twenty workers selected from various divisions of Nihon Tabi K.K. began producing prototype tires on February 22, 1930. The imported machinery was only for forming and vulcanizing. All of the other operations were done by hand. Making the task even more challenging was the fledgling tiremaker's initial inexperience. No one at the company had any previous experience in tire production and so a 10-page instruction booklet, shipped with the equipment, served as the company's only technical expertise.

Not surprisingly, the wheels turned slowly at first. Four months passed before the first tire was actually created. The 29 x 4.5 four-ply tire that finally emerged from the plant would become very popular on the Fords, Chryslers, and Chevrolets traveling Japan's roadways.

Along with perfecting its product, the new company needed a name. Those first tire molds ordered from Akron had to be engraved during their fabrication with a brand name or the name of the manufacturer. The company didn't want to use its tire operations' official name, Nihon Tabi K.K., Tire Department, given the preference in Japan for foreign imports, especially those from the United States and Britain. Virtually all passenger cars and trucks on the road in Japan at the time were imported and used foreign-made tires. It was assumed that automobile owners wanted the quality and image associated with imported tires.

So the shoe company began the search for an English name to get its tire business started on the right foot.

Traditionally, tire brands were taken from an inventor or company founder's name, as with Harvey Firestone, J. B. Dunlop, Charles Goodyear, and B. F. Goodrich. With an interesting twist, Nihon Tabi followed this tire industry tradition.

The direct translation of Ishibashi's family name was "stone bridge." Company officials were not satisfied with the sound of "Stonebridge." By reversing the syllables, however, you got "Bridgestone"—a name with a tough, durable, international sound.

With a new name and 10 pages of tire-building know-how, Bridgestone rolled into history.

Ironically, Firestone filed a trademark suit in Japan against the company that would one day share its name. Bridgestone eventually won the judgment on the grounds that the word was actually a translation of the founder's name, even if the syllables had been reversed.

Radical Radial Market Changes

Just 10 years down the road from its founding in 1930, Bridgestone tires were rolling off the line at the massive plant in Yokohama, Japan.
(Bridgestone Corporation Archives)

The globalization of the tire industry during the late '80s can be traced directly to the introduction of radial tires almost 35 years earlier. First introduced to the French replacement market in 1954, radials offered substantial advantages over the bias tire in both wear and fuel economy. By 1958, they were original equipment on French-made cars. Soon after, they were rolled out and adopted throughout Europe.

So dramatic was the radial difference, they inevitably replaced bias-ply tires in every nation they were introduced. In 1975, approximately 60 percent of all tires sold in the United States were bias tires and 40 percent were radials. By 1980, essentially all new tires being sold were radials.

Radials' relentless march to market dominance had a dramatic effect on the tire industry. Changing over to radial production required billions of dollars of capital investments at a time when the tire replacement market was shrinking because the new radial tire lasted 50 percent longer.

The impact was immediate and profound. When the shakeout sparked by radials ended, the world's tire-making borders had been completely redrawn. In just a three-year period, these radical changes were created:

- Germany's Continental AG purchased American General Tire in 1987;
- Japan's Bridgestone merged with Firestone in 1988;
- Italy's Pirelli acquired the United States Armstrong Tire in 1988;
- Japan's Yokohoma bought Mohawk in 1989; and
- France's Michelin bought U.S.-based Uniroyal Goodrich in 1989.

For a long time, the only American Company that did not take part in the urge to merge was Goodyear Tire & Rubber Company. That changed in early 1999 when it acquired control over the U.S. and European assets of Sumitomo Rubber Industries Ltd. of Japan.

Key players in the Bridgestone/ Firestone merger, Firestone Chairman John Nevin and Bridgestone's Akira Yeiri, greet one another during a welcome party in Tokyo on June 7, 1988, three months after the two companies came together.
(Bridgestone/Firestone Collection)

Wheeling and Dealing

When Firestone and Bridgestone came together as a single company in 1988, the deal was worth $2.6 billion, with Bridgestone paying $80 for each outstanding share of Firestone stock. Prior to that agreement, Italy's Pirelli had made an offer to Firestone of $58 per share. Bridgestone Corporation's President Akira Yeiri decided to make a counter offer and consulted with Bridgestone honorary chairman Kanichiro Ishibashi regarding the details. Ishibashi firmly supported Yeiri's decision, and the board of directors approved the deal on March 14, 1988. Not surprisingly, 99.4 percent of the votes cast at a special meeting of the Firestone shareholders favored the Bridgestone deal.

As the 1990s drew to a close, so did any criticism of the merger. The newly combined corporation was outperforming either of its predecessor companies. Bridgestone/Firestone, Inc. announced record sales and net earnings for 1998. Sales reached $7.4 billion, compared with $7.1 billion in 1997.

Financials aside, it was quite clear that the combined companies could do things neither could dream of doing alone. The most dramatic example of this new potential was the company's combined impact on automobile racing, where each name brought something different to the track, whether it be in the Americas, Asia or Europe.

Seven-Year Courtship

Firestone chairman John Nevin and his Bridgestone counterpart, Akira Yeiri, were architects of the merger. Before combining their companies, the two had built a relationship while discussing various business deals seven years earlier. On March 17, 1988, just two hours before the Firestone board met to consider the Bridgestone $80 per share offer, Yeiri paid a visit to Nevin's office.

"I verbally assured him that Bridgestone would have the full support of Firestone's management if the merger was completed, and handed him a letter requesting that Bridgestone submit a formal offer to acquire Firestone," Nevin said. "Without those verbal assurances, and that letter, Bridgestone may not have proceeded with its planned tender offer.

"I can make that statement without equivocation, because Akira Yeiri came to my office on March 17, 1988, as a respected and valued friend, not as a stranger."

Bridgestone's 1983 acquisition of the Firestone plant in LaVergne, Tennessee, would ultimately lead to the merger of the two companies. (Bridgestone/Firestone Collection)

Global Urge to Merge

Bridgestone had long been Japan's leading tire company. Its tires accounted for approximately 50 percent of all sales in the Japanese original equipment and replacement markets and enjoyed a reputation for design and manufacturing excellence. However, its market dominance was threatened. Japanese automobile manufacturers building cars in North America tended to obtain tires in the host country.

Nevin reasoned that Bridgestone's future growth depended upon deeper penetration of the U.S. market, a move best accomplished by joint ventures or the acquisition of a U.S. tire company. Firestone, in the meantime, was recovering from a recall of the steel-belted 500 model tire. Nevin knew that Firestone could benefit from Bridgestone's quality control and financial strength. He believed an alliance was a good move for both companies.

According to Nevin, the men and women working for Firestone greeted the Bridgestone venture "with an enthusiasm that in some cases approached euphoria." With little overlap existing between the two companies' tire operations, they reasoned that their jobs would be far more secure. They also realized the combined company offered significantly greater opportunities than going it alone in the increasingly competitive global tire market.

In addition, since Bridgestone didn't produce synthetic rubber in the United States, the merger gave Firestone facilities the opportunity to supply synthetics to Bridgestone plants as well as provide additional production capacity in Canada and South America. In the case of

RIDING IN STYLE

Six years after he founded the Bridgestone Corporation in 1930, Shojiro Ishibashi purchased an American motorcar that reflected his personal taste for superior craftsmanship—a prominent luxury car of its day—the Lincoln Zephyr. Ironically, or perhaps prophetically, the Zephyr came equipped with the premier American tire of its day crafted by Firestone.

The 1936 Lincoln Zephyr remained in the Ishibashi family through the next several decades, although it was remodeled to serve as the Bridgestone company fire engine. Eventually, the Zephyr fire engine was retired, and the car was put back to its original design, painted its factory-issued black and installed black leatherette upholstery.

Shojiro Ishibashi (right) stands with other Bridgestone Corporation officials on that day in 1936 when the Lincoln-Zephyr was delivered. Sixty-three years later, the car is still in the same family.

(Hiroshi Ishibashi, Bridgestone Corporation)

In 1996, as a tribute to his father, Kanichiro Ishibashi decided to restore the family heirloom to its original gleaming condition. He enlisted the help of many friends and organizations, including the Ford Motor Company, which was the car's original manufacturer. Before the project was completed however, Kanichiro Ishibashi became ill and died June 30, 1997. His son, Hiroshi Ishibashi, also a part of the Bridgestone Corporation, then took over the restoration project as a promise to his father and grandfather. Overseeing the cleaning, reproducing, re-tooling and re-painting, Ishibashi made sure the car's luster and bold lines were restored to top condition.

Far more than simply transporting the company's founding family or supporting the business through its use as a fire engine, this Lincoln Zephyr brought together Ford, Firestone and Bridgestone—three companies whose relationship proved critical in the passing century.

In the Lincoln-Zephyr restoration project, the car was painted a deep Zephyr Blue, making it truly reborn.

(Hiroshi Ishibashi, Bridgestone Corporation)

air springs, the merger brought together Bridgestone's strong position in the Japanese market with Firestone's strong position in North America. With the rubber-roofing business, the new relationship offered expanded sales opportunities in Japan's developing market for these products. Finally, the merger gave Bridgestone the chance to increase its appeal and awareness in the United States by selling Bridgestone-branded tires in Firestone's automotive tire and service stores.

Nashville Mayor Phil Bredesen, Bridgestone's Yoichiro Kaizaki, and Tennessee Governor Ned McWherter are all smiles as they meet to dedicate the new Nashville-based Bridgestone/ Firestone Headquarters.
(Bridgestone/Firestone Collection)

Getting Things Rolling

Bridgestone and Firestone officials barely paused to celebrate the historic merger before beginning the formidable task of combining two very large organizations. Although built on the same core beliefs, the companies operated under vastly different corporate cultures.

As Bridgestone executives toured Firestone factories to get a closer look at the facilities their company had acquired, they quickly realized the road ahead would be more difficult than first perceived. Firestone's investments to update its factories had been insufficient and even more dramatic was the company's financial state. There was a time in the early 1990s when Bridgestone/Firestone, Inc. was losing an astonishing $1 million a day.

Instead of panicking and looking for stopgap remedies, Bridgestone/Firestone developed a long-term strategy and stuck with it, even during difficult times. The first step in the plan was to ensure Firestone product quality by updating the factories. The company invested $1.5 billion in new plant equipment and employee training. This investment took several years to bear fruit, but it was an essential first step.

While the factories were being modernized, Yoichiro Kaizaki, appointed Bridgestone/Firestone chairman and CEO in 1991, began re-creating the company, transforming it into a leaner, more agile organization. He eliminated multiple layers of management and created 21 operating divisions. Each was accountable for its individual business sector, reporting directly to the office of the CEO and President. Significantly, Kaizaki also combined the Bridgestone and Firestone tire sales organizations to create a unified marketing approach rather than forcing head-to-head competition between brands under the same corporate umbrella.

As part of the overall reorganization in 1992, Firestone's headquarters moved from Akron, Ohio, to create the North American headquarters for the combined company in Nashville, Tennessee. The move played a pivotal role in converting Bridgestone/Firestone from the co-existence of two organizations into a single, unified company with a common mission. Kaizaki was rewarded for his efforts in 1993 by being named president, chairman and CEO of Bridgestone/Firestone's parent company, Bridgestone Corporation in Japan.

The next critical step in the long-term plan was to establish a multi-brand, multi-channel marketing strategy. Led by Shu Ishibashi, then director of consumer tires marketing and later promoted to vice president of consumer tires marketing, this approach addressed the question plaguing all tire manufacturers: How do you keep independent dealers happy while business grows in other emerging channels such as the mass merchandisers, discount chains, and warehouse clubs?

The multi-channeled approach involved developing different tire products for the various channels to minimize conflict in the marketplace. The company's newest technol-

Poised for a new millennium, Bridgestone/Firestone's company-owned retail stores continue to create a friendly public face for the brand, and a retail laboratory for testing the ideas it will later share with independent dealers.
(Bridgestone/Firestone Collection)

ogy products were identified as "core products" reserved for the "Family Channel" made up of company-owned stores and independent dealers. The dealers, who still account for the majority of tire sales, were extremely pleased with this new approach and helped Bridgestone/Firestone achieve dramatic sales growth.

The multi-brand part of the strategy required developing a clear market position for each of the company's brands. Bridgestone was targeted at brand-conscious consumers looking for premium tires while the Firestone brand was positioned to address the needs of the more value-conscious. Dayton and other associate brands were aimed at price-conscious consumers.

Imitation is the sincerest form of flattery. The multi-brand, multi-channel strategy proved so successful that it was copied by other major tire companies in the mid-to-late '90s.

Racing Revival

When they toured the country following the merger, Bridgestone/Firestone executives asked longtime Firestone dealers what it would take to return the brand to its former prominence. The answer came loud and clear: Return to Indy car racing.

Focusing on Family

Kanichiro Ishibashi, son of Bridgestone Corporation's founder, served the company through its many phases. (Bridgestone Corporation)

Harvey S. Firestone, Jr. (left) and Elizabeth Firestone enjoy exhibits and arts at the 1933 Chicago World's Fair with their father, Harvey S. Firestone, Sr., an entrepreneur and devout family man.
(Russ Vitale Photography)

Harvey S. Firestone and Shojiro Ishibashi were successes in every sense of the word. Their accomplishments extended beyond business to embrace family life.

Ishibashi married Masako on May 5, 1917, and together they had two sons and four daughters. He led his family by example and through his values.

"It has always been my way to maintain my ideals, to live and exert myself in a manner true to my convictions, and to push ahead on the straight-and-narrow path," Shojiro Ishibashi wrote in 1962.

In both cases the founders' sons followed in their fathers' footsteps, coming up in the family business, making sure that their practices, in both their private and professional lives, echoed that of their parents'.

"I remember my father as a man of infinite patience. He always had time for his children. He imparted to us the simple, fundamental precepts of honesty and integrity which guided his life and which, God willing, will always serve to guide the Firestone organization throughout the years to come," said Harvey S. Firestone, Jr.

From its headquarters in Tokyo, Bridgestone Corporation serves the world as the company rolls into the next millennium now a truly global company with retail, research and manufacturing facilities in more than 18 countries. (Bridgestone Corporation Archives)

The company took the dealer recommendation to heart. Top executives experienced first hand what Firestone had been missing with a visit to the brickyard in 1992. Then in 1993, the company announced Firestone would return to the arena that helped establish the brand as a driving force in the first half of the 20th century. Supported by the theme "The Legend Returns," Firestone returned to Indy car racing with a vengeance.

The impact was immediate. Before driver Scott Pruett and the Patrick Racing Team turned their first test lap in 1994, and before the first Firestone-equipped car competed in its first race in 1995, Firestone sales rocketed upward. It was as if a huge reservoir of enthusiasm contained since the '70s and '80s while Firestone was struggling, poured forth from longtime, loyal Firestone dealers. The dealers were re-energized. The key players in tire marketing now had hard, tangible evidence that the company was committed to supporting the Firestone name.

Hitting 90 and Speeding Ahead

Under the leadership of Bridgestone/ Firestone Chairman and CEO Masatoshi Ono and President Kenji Shibata, the company's long-term plans began to have even more focus in the late '90s. The company direction followed the parallel paths of technology and motorsports.

Bridgestone/Firestone relied on Research & Development centers in Tokyo, Akron, and Rome to roll out advanced tire technologies, such as UNI-T® and UNI-T AQ.™ Consumers wanted and were willing to pay a premium for these practical advances. The fact that the company competed at motorsports' highest levels worldwide promoted its technologies and products, while at the same time serving to help develop new technologies. In addition, various racing segments helped differentiate the brands' characteristics and its consumer.

Even in this high-tech age, tire-building is still a craft to Bridgestone/Firestone. The company's tires are a reflection of the superior quality and dedication of the company's 45,000-member employee family.
(Bridgestone/Firestone Collection)

Bridgestone/Firestone was on a roll and its momentum led the U.S. tire industry in the second half of the '90s. The company more than doubled production in its North American plants. Still it couldn't keep up with demand. Firestone became the fastest-growing consumer tire brand in America. The "Fire" was back!

Meanwhile, the company also established strategic alliances with major truck manufacturers and fleets and saw its truck tire business boom. Bridgestone/Firestone continued to strengthen its relationships with truck dealers—relationships built on value-added service and quality products. The company also experienced solid growth in Canada, Latin America, and in its non-tire divisions.

Looking Down the Road

We come to the close of the Firestone century—the first one, at any rate.

We hope you agree, it's been quite a ride. An unbelievable ride, really. Who would have thought a business born of a horse and buggy race could traverse a century so successfully and move into the next century as one of the world's most recognizable names?

Unlike the typical tire, Firestone has made the long trip much better for all the wear; much better for the growing pains that quickly followed the first discoveries; much better for the economic, political, product and management challenges faced over the first century; much better for weaving in and out and back again on the racetrack; for having served the world through global military conflicts and financial depression; for having entertained the world with everything from motorsports to monumental musical artists; for the failures as well as the successes; for having merged to emerge at the new millennium a truly global company; much better for having been tempered and tested by time.

Each tire crafted by Bridgestone/Firestone is manually inspected before it makes its way to the consumer.
(Bridgestone/Firestone Collection)

We've come a long way. Firestone has changed as the world changed around it, with it and, in some cases, because of it. Firestone is a far different company today from what it was in the past. In fact, Firestone, as it was founded a

Despite the high degree of automation at the Bridgestone/Firestone plant in Warren County, Tennessee, threading the golden steel tire cord still requires meticulous hand operation.
(Bridgestone/Firestone Collection)

At the Warren County Plant in Tennessee, an employee sorts and labels bus tires in the final inspection department.
(Bridgestone/Firestone Collection)

century ago, no longer exists as an independent company. Some might even suggest that since the Bridgestone merger, Firestone has ceased to exist at all. But nothing is farther from the truth. Firestone not only exists, it stands for something in the minds of its makers, dealers, and customers all over the world. It has evolved to become part of something bigger. Few could make this 100-year ride alone.

Firestone hasn't done it alone. Traveling through the 20th century, it's made plenty of friends—from U.S. presidents to noted international performers, from the age's foremost inventors to its fastest drivers, from a network of loyal dealers who share an uncommon dedication to more than 45,000 employee family members in the Americas who share a powerful vision, from renowned celebrities to the average man and woman on the street. Firestone has 100 years' worth of acquaintances to its credit.

So what lies ahead? We can only imagine. Bridgestone/Firestone tires. Better rubbers and new materials compounded for climate and road conditions using more recycled materials. Completely computerized tire systems that literally make Firestone tires one-stop shops that regulate, service, and repair themselves. Tires that no longer require inflation or may not even be filled with air. E-commerce will deliver more tires, more quickly, while tires transport man faster and far more safely. Tire companies will take mankind beyond its automotive needs with ongoing contributions to home, culture, and global prosperity.

Firestone has emerged, as one century ends and another begins, as much more than a tire and rubber company. It has become an entity that takes people where they want to go, whether it is a physical place in space by way of a great product or a place in life by means of a superior philosophy.

We could go on and on, because there seems to be no end to the need, no end to the ideas, and no end to the road that races before us.

We hope you look down the road and view the new millennium, as we do, with optimism. Because optimism is the prerequisite to invention.

A line of inspectors – such as these employees at Bridgestone/Firestone's Warren County plant – manually examine the tire's quality.
(Bridgestone/Firestone Collection)

BRIDGESTONE/FIRESTONE BOARD OF DIRECTORS

Tetsuo Ando

Gary Crigger

Mark A. Emkes

Minekazu Fujimura

Yoichiro Kaizaki

John Lampe

Masatoshi Ono

Charles R. Ramsey

Kenji Shibata

Arthur Stuart

As the company enters the year 2000, the leadership of Bridgestone/Firestone, Inc. supports the strong heritage of ingenuity and dedication to quality service and products that began with a "fire" in 1900.

(Bridgestone/Firestone Collection)

1868

December 20 – Harvey S. Firestone is born on a farm near Columbiana, Ohio.

1900

There are now eight rubber and elastics establishments in Akron with a total of 2,677 wage earners collectively earning $1 million. The industry has been growing since B.F. Goodrich's Akron factory opened in 1870. It was the first rubber-manufacturing plant west of the Alleghenies.

August 3 – The Firestone Tire & Rubber Company is founded in Akron, Ohio. The capital stock is only $50,000 ($20,000 in cash and $30,000 in patents). In addition, Firestone introduces the solid rubber sidewire tire as one of the first Firestone products.

December 27 – Harvey S. Firestone, Jr., the four-year-old son of the founder, is lifted in the air to pull the engine switch that puts the first Firestone factory into operation.

1903

Firestone begins producing its own tires for the first time.

1904

By late summer, Firestone develops the first mechanically fastened, straight-sided pneumatic automobile tire.

October 8 – The first angular non-skid tread is introduced with the words "Firestone Non-Skid" molded diagonally across the tread. Its name is explained in an advertisement of the day's issue of *Motor Age*, "Thus the name prevents the slip...The letters of the words form more angles and points of contact than any other non-skid tread. The spaces between the letters cause just the right amount of suction to grip the slippery road and prevent the side slipping." All highway tires produced after this product will use tread patterns for traction.

1909

Firestone begins manufacturing tire rims.

1910

Profits for The Firestone Tire & Rubber Company exceed $1 million for the first time.

1911

May 30 – The inaugural Indianapolis 500 is won on Firestone tires by driver Ray Harroun.

June 8 – Plant 1, Firestone's new factory in Akron, opens.

1905

The automobile is making news and automobile registrations reach 77,000 nationwide. Ransom E. Olds begins mass production of his products while Henry Ford is abandoning expensive touring cars for lower-priced runabouts. The Glidden Tours, sponsored by machine age enthusiast Charles J. Glidden of Brookline, Mass., popularize long-distance driving. Glidden offers an annual trophy, not for speed, but for the best performance.

1906

Firestone delivers 2,000 sets of tires to the Ford Motor Company. It is the largest single order for tires placed by the auto industry to date. Annual tire sales exceed $1 million for the first time in the company's history.

1907

Firestone develops the first commercial "demountable rim" allowing easy repair and replacement of tires by the general public.

1908

January 19 – John W. Thomas is the first chemist hired by the company. Firestone now has a research and development department. Prior to this, it was said that the R&D department was in the "head and hands" of founder Harvey S. Firestone. Thomas later became president of the company (1932-1941) and ultimately chairman of the board (1941-1946).

October 1 – The Model T Ford makes its first appearance.

Ford Motor Company
Detroit, U.S.A. JUN 11 1908 B 1718
Pay to the order of Firestone Tire & Rubber Co $110526 85/100
One hundred ten thousand five hundred twenty six and 85/100 Dollars
IN SETTLEMENT OF ACCOUNT AS STATED ON THE BACK OF THIS CHECK
To Corn Exchange Bank, Grand Central Branch, New York.
Ford Motor Company
James Couzens, Treasurer

1912

July 13 – The rumor that Firestone will merge with Goodyear Tire and Rubber becomes so persistent that a strong denial is issued.

1915

July – The first issue of the employee newspaper, The Firestone Non-Skid, is published for 5,000 company employees worldwide. The premiere issue celebrates a company on the move. The four-page paper includes articles on a new Firestone Clubhouse, new additions to the main plant, company picnics, workplace safety and the standings of the Firestone baseball league.

1916

The year some called "the year of the employee." The eight-hour workday is inaugurated by Firestone, the Firestone Bank is started (originally called Rubber City Savings Bank), and Firestone Park, a new community for company employees, is opened.

Three friends, Harvey S. Firestone, Thomas Edison and Henry Ford, set out for the first of many camping trips. Oftentimes they camped with others including John Burroughs, their wives and children, or American presidents.

1918

Harvey S. Firestone begins the pioneering "Ship by Truck" movement. The campaign jump starts the development of the trucking industry. This is also the year in which free life insurance for employees is offered.

1919

Ohio becomes the leading state in every branch of the tire industry and in the manufacture of automobile casings and rubber inner tubes. It also has more rubber workers than any other state, 63,637. Firestone adds a new mechanical building and a Steel Products plant. Its line of plants, which extends for more than a mile, is linked together by more than six miles of interplant railroad and a 70-ton locomotive. The company now has its own rail line to move raw materials and finished products.

July 13– Lieutenant Colonel Dwight D. Eisenhower, a member of the Army's first Transcontinental Motortruck Convoy, stops for a chicken dinner on the lawn at the Firestone Homestead near Columbiana, Ohio.

1920

Firestone perfected a method of insulating tire cords against internal heat called "gum-dipping." Also for the first time, Firestone has its first 5 million tire production year.

May 31 – Gaston Chevrolet wins the Indy 500 on a set of Firestone tires. For the first time ever, the winner uses only one set of tires. The feat will be repeated 41 races later when A. J. Foyt does it again using Firestone tires.

November 29 – Ex-president William Howard Taft, on a speaking tour to discuss the League of Nations, arrives in Akron and visits with Harvey S. Firestone. It underscores the fact that Firestone has become an important figure in national affairs.

1922

Harvey S. Firestone organizes a protest against the Stevenson Rubber Restriction Scheme and the British rubber cartels. He advocates that "Americans should produce their own rubber."

1928

Firestone's first overseas tire manufacturing plant opens in Brentford, England. The company is quickly transforming itself from an American to an international operation.

October 24 - Harvey S. Firestone is voted one of nine "Pioneers of American Industry," by 1,700 industrial leaders. Other pioneers include Henry Ford, Orville Wright, George Eastman and Thomas Edison.

December 3 - The first commercially sponsored musical program on radio, the *Voice of Firestone*, goes on the air.

1930

The Depression hits the automobile industry and along with it, the tire business. Firestone sales begin a 5-year decline.

January 28 – On the golf links at Ormond Beach, after Harvey S. Firestone makes a long putt, John D. Rockefeller, the richest man in the world, presents him with a dime. The story and photograph receive national attention.

1925

April 5 – Factory production of the industry's first low-pressure balloon tire begins. This breakthrough is made possible by incorporating the gum-dipping process. Balloon tires offer the average motorist extraordinary mileage.

May 30 – Peter DePaolo wins the grueling Indianapolis 500 on Firestone balloon tires, exceeding 100 miles per hour for the first time in the race's history.

July 18 – A new stadium of steel and concrete designed to be as good as any for the professionals is dedicated in Akron for use by the Firestone industrial league team and its opponents. It seats 4,000 people.

August 3 – The first quarter-century of The Firestone Tire & Rubber Company is marked. The company occupies 3,345,407 square feet of floor space and will have sales of $125,597,998 for the year. In a report on its 25th anniversary, the Firestone organization depicts itself to the world as one that is "powerful, alert and closely knit" which "is able to meet changing conditions as quickly as the small business, with the added advantage of the men, machines and money of the modern industrial organization."

October 14 – Harvey S. Firestone announces the completion of an agreement with the Liberian Government by which the Firestone Plantation Company obtains a 99-year lease of one million acres of land suitable for rubber-growing.

1926

Firestone initiates the one-stop service store program, eventually called the Firestone Tire & Service Center.

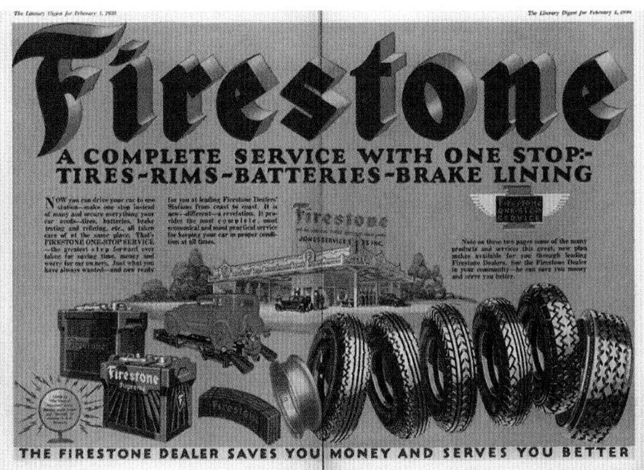

Firestone negotiates lease of jungle acreage and transforms it into a rubber plantation.

On the second green Mr. Firestone made a remarkably long putt and received the Rockefeller dime.—World Wide Photos.

1932

Firestone develops the first practical low-pressure pneumatic tractor tire and begins the "Put the Farm on Rubber" campaign.

1935

Firestone's sales enjoy a remarkable turnaround. Sales, which began to slump in 1930, went from $144 million to $120 to $84 to $75 million before starting to rebound, ending up at $121 million in 1935.

1938

February 7 – Harvey S. Firestone dies in his sleep early in the morning at his vacation home in Miami Beach.

1940

As the clouds of war gather in Europe and Asia, and the need for a natural rubber substitute looms ever larger with the possibility that natural rubber shipments from Africa and Asia will be cut off, Firestone produces synthetic rubber. The company develops and begins manufacturing special tires for combat vehicles and other military items.

May 30 – Wilbur Shaw drives to victory in the Indy 500 on a set of tires made from synthetic rubber. With this win the legendary Wilbur Shaw becomes the first driver to win the race three times. All three wins – 1937, 1939 and 1940 – are on Firestone tires.

August 3 – In celebration of its 40th anniversary, Firestone uses the New York World's Fair to publicly display, for the first time, the process by which synthetic rubber is manufactured. The public's fascination with this "miracle of science" is such that many come to the Fair, now in its second year, just to witness the process for themselves. The World's Fair exhibit features actual tire manufacturing and a working farm, complete with animals and farm hands.

1950

August 3 – The company celebrates its 50th birthday. A monument to Harvey S. Firestone is unveiled, next to the Research Building in Akron, by his sons. Harvey S. Firestone, Jr., tells the nation on The *Voice of Firestone*, "In those 50 years, our company has grown from a small to a worldwide organization with more than 70,000 people." At the time of the 50th anniversary, the war in Korea is underway and Firestone is very much part of the war effort. In Fall River, Massachusetts, The Firestone Rubber & Latex Products Company makes gas masks. In Akron, Plant 3 is devoted to defense products and is expanded so that Firestone is ranked as one of the principal producers of 57mm and 75mm recoilless rifles for ground forces. The tire plant in Memphis, Tennessee, produces bridge floats and other gear.

1951

Firestone begins producing the Corporal guided missile for the government at the Los Angeles plant.

1953

The Firestone "500," an all-nylon tubeless tire, is introduced for high-speed passenger car travel.

December 31– The company achieves $1 billion in sales for the first time – $1,029,402,035 to be exact. Firestone's defense business is at its peak.

1942

Firestone is the first to produce synthetic rubber in a government-owned plant.

1943

November 29– Firestone becomes the first company to regularly present a television program, *Firestone Televues*. The first show features an interview by NBC President Niles Trammel of Harvey S. Firestone, Jr. On the same night the *Voice of Firestone* celebrated its 15th radio anniversary.

1945

August 3 – As the company turns 45, World War II is ending. The company has made extraordinary contributions to the war effort, including synthetic rubber and a variety of products that can also be used in post-war times.

1948

May 31 – Firestone Tires win the 25th Indianapolis 500 in a row. Four of the Firestone brothers are on hand to congratulate Mauri Rose on his victory.

The *Voice of Firestone* radio program is simulcast on television. It is the first coast-to-coast musical telecast on NBC.

1949

Jim Roper pilots his Lincoln to victory in the first NASCAR Winston Cup race on Firestone tires.

1954

May 3 – For the first time, the *Voice of Firestone* is telecast in color.

February 22– President Dwight D. Eisenhower sends Congress a report titled "A 10 Year National Highway Program." The report, by a presidential Commission headed by General Lucius Clay, recommends creation of a Federal Highway Corporation to finance a $101 billion program, including $25 billion for the Interstate System. To pay for the Interstate System, the corporation would issue $20 billion in long term bonds. The President calls the plan "a solid foundation for a sound program." However, it fails in Congress.

1955

May 31 – Producing at a rate of one million pounds of rubber a day, Firestone becomes the world's largest rubber producer upon purchasing the government's synthetic rubber plants in Akron, Ohio, and Lake Charles, Louisiana.

1956

June 29 – President Eisenhower signs the Federal Aid Highway Act of 1956, ushering in the Interstate era. The idea of a true national system of highways, which had been so appealing to Eisenhower and Firestone in 1919, has now come to fruition.

1957

A 7.7-mile proving-grounds in Fort Stockton, Texas, is developed by Firestone to test tires under actual driving conditions, but in a controlled environment. Firestone develops a high-speed race tire to withstand speeds in excess of 190 miles per hour for the first running of the International 500-mile race at Monza, Italy. Jimmy Bryan won the first race on Firestones at a world record of 160.057 miles per hour.

1958

August 15 – Company president Raymond C. Firestone announces the development of "Diene," a synthetic rubber, and partial replacement for natural rubber, which makes tires more crack-resistant, reduces running temperatures and improves skid resistance.

1959

During the year, the company bestows its 10,000th 20-year service watch, an indication of the loyalty of the Firestone employees. The company now has a total of 71 plants in 19 countries.

1960

September – *Dun's Review*, a business magazine, picks Firestone as one of the ten best managed companies in the nation.

1961

Firestone acquires Dayton Tire.

1962

June 22 – Firestone joins 85 leading American companies in embracing the "Plan for Progress" which disavows employment discrimination because of race, creed, color or national origin.

1963

June 16 – The final *Voice of Firestone* television program airs, featuring Arthur Fiedler as the principal conductor.

1969

July 20 – Two U.S. astronauts, Neil Armstrong and Edwin Aldrin, land the lunar module Eagle on the moon. Raymond C. Firestone notes, "Our success in landing a man on the moon should prove to us that this nation can solve its problems–of pollution, the human and physical problems of the ghettos, and our rising traffic toll."

1970

August 3 – Now ranked in the top 50 American corporations (at number 37), on this 70th anniversary, sales for the fiscal year are the highest ever – $2.28 billion, an increase of 21,000 times over the revenues of $110,000 during 1901, the first full year of operations. The diversification of the company has accelerated to areas ranging from coated fabrics to footwear.

1971

Firestone introduces the first American-made Steel Belt Radial Tire.

July 23 – William Tubman, President of the African nation of Liberia, dies, ending a 45-year relationship with the Firestone family and company. Tubman met Harvey S. Firestone when he was a Senator and Firestone was in Liberia to begin planting rubber trees there. Tubman was one of several Liberian officials who attempted to secure a $5 million loan from the U.S. Government to help his country bolster its lagging economy. The federal government turned him down so Firestone loaned Liberia the money and trees were planted.

1972

June 18 - Ray Elder produces the 568th Firestone win in NASCAR when he takes the checkered flag at Riverside Raceway.

August– The *Detroit Free Press* reports that President Richard Nixon's new, custom Lincoln Continental will be equipped with Transport 500 Wide Oval Firestone tires. A tradition is maintained, as every Presidential limousine since the early Franklin Roosevelt era has been equipped with Firestone tires.

1973

June 1 – Harvey S. Firestone, Jr., eldest son of the company founder, dies at the age of 75. The successful stewardship of Harvey S. Firestone's sons is underscored by the fact that this year is the company's first $3 billion year in sales.

1964

Firestone introduces and begins producing radial ply passenger tires for replacement use on lightweight American and European cars.

August 13 – Firestone President Raymond C. Firestone attends the bill signing by President Lyndon B. Johnson for the $2.4 billion Federal Aid Highway Act of 1964. He is a strong advocate for the bill which advances transportation. It parallels his father's support of the "Ship by Truck" and "Good Roads" movements of the early part of the century.

1965

Firestone introduces the "Super Sports Wide Oval" tire. Called the "Shape of the Future," the tire is readily accepted by auto manufacturers as original equipment on many 1967 high-performance cars. This concept of wide, low-profile tires for high-performance cars continues throughout the century.

Driving his 17,500-horsepower jet streamliner, the "Green Monster," Art Arfons of Akron, Ohio, sets a new world land speed record of 576.553 miles per hour at the Bonneville, Utah, Salt Flats. The "Green Monster" is equipped with Firestone tires and wheels.

August 3 – The company celebrates its 65th anniversary with the largest annual sales in the history of the company – a record $1.45 billion generated by employees in 23 countries. It makes and markets 3,600 types and sizes of tires as well as 2,000 other products in the fields of rubber, metals, plastics, synthetics, textiles and chemicals. The tire division of the Seiberling Tire Company is acquired.

1968

January 1 – Firestone will become one of the nation's major seatbelt suppliers and will be in the forefront of developing passive restraint systems, as law requires all new cars to have seatbelts.

December 20 – On the 100th anniversary of the birth of Harvey S. Firestone, Sr., his son, Harvey Jr., is honorary chairman of The Firestone Tire & Rubber Company, and Raymond C. Firestone is chairman and chief executive officer. 1968 sales reach the $2 billion mark for the first time.

Graham Hill becomes the first driver to win the FIA Formula One championship on Firestone tires.

October 17– Arab nations begin an oil embargo against the United States in an attempt to raise prices and alter U.S. support of Israel. This begins a series of consequences which will impact Firestone and other American tire makers for years to come. People are driving less and not as far, the demand for smaller European and Japanese cars goes up, and the imports tend to have tires with labels like Michelin and Bridgestone.

November 1 – Raymond C. Firestone relinquishes his post as chief executive officer to Richard A. Riley. He remains as Chairman of the Board.

1974

The first steel radial with run-flat capability is introduced by Firestone. The steel Radial 500 ACT (Advanced Concept Tire), makes it possible for a car with a flat tire to be driven more than 50 miles on the highway at speeds averaging 40 miles per hour.

1975

August 3 – The company is 75 and, despite decades of success, steps out of motorsports. However, Firestone has grown into a multi-billion-dollar, diversified, international manufacturing and merchandising enterprise. It operates in 28 countries on six continents, has rubber plantations on three continents and sales operations throughout the world. "The 75th anniversary of The Firestone Tire & Rubber Company," Raymond C. Firestone, Chairman, writes to employees, "is a time to reflect on what has made this a great and successful company. What I think it comes down to is people working together."

1976

September 30– Raymond C. Firestone steps down as the Chairman of the Board of The Firestone Tire & Rubber Co. three weeks after turning 68, the mandatory retirement age for directors. He was the last of founder Harvey S. Firestone's five sons to have a management role in the company. He joined Firestone in 1933, after graduating from Princeton University, and held a variety of positions in sales, and production and research before becoming company Chairman in 1966.

1978

May 19 to July 10 – Hearings on the safety of Firestone steel-belted radial 500 tires by the House committee on Interstate and Foreign Commerce are conducted.

November – In the biggest product recall in the nation's history at the time, Firestone recalls 400,000 Firestone 500 steel-belted radial tires. The result is a cost of $148.3 million for Firestone.

1979

Firestone introduces the temporary spare, which allows more trunk space and reduces fuel consumption by reducing weight.

June 30 – The company announces that it has replaced more than 3.1 million tires in the "500" recall program. The total includes 2.4 million replaced free and slightly more than 700,000 on a half-price or partial payment basis. More than 2.8 million letters have been mailed to registered owners of eligible tires or of vehicles that may have been equipped with them when new. A press release issued by Firestone later in the year sums it up, "The worldwide press coverage the recall received made it one of the most publicized news events in business history."

December 1– John Nevin joins Firestone as president.

1983

A revolution is complete as U.S. automakers now exclusively equip all new cars with radial tires. By contrast, in 1971 radial tires made up only 2 percent of sales to Detroit automakers.

Bridgestone acquires the LaVergne, Tennessee, plant from Firestone.

1987

April 30 – Firestone's Board of Directors announces that the corporate headquarters will move to Chicago from Akron.

1988

February – Bridgestone and Firestone announce a tire manufacturing joint venture.

March 7 – Pirelli S.P.A. offers to buy all outstanding shares of common stock in the Firestone Tire & Rubber Company for $58 per share.

March 21 – The Bridgestone Corporation formally offers to buy all outstanding shares of common stock in The Firestone Tire & Rubber Company for $80 per share. The offer is approved a few weeks later by 99.4 percent of the votes cast at a special meeting of Firestone's shareholders.

1991

Bridgestone/Firestone announces the Affiliated Dealer Program, which helps smaller dealers compete against larger national retailers. This marks a turning point in the company's relations with independent dealers and sets the stage for additional dealer-related programs which help fuel steady market share growth in the '90s.

May 16 – Bridgestone Corporation announces it will increase its investment in Bridgestone/Firestone by a total of $1.4 billion.

Firestone becomes the official tire of the Indy Lights Championship series.

1992

Bridgestone/Firestone corporate headquarters moves to Nashville.

1989

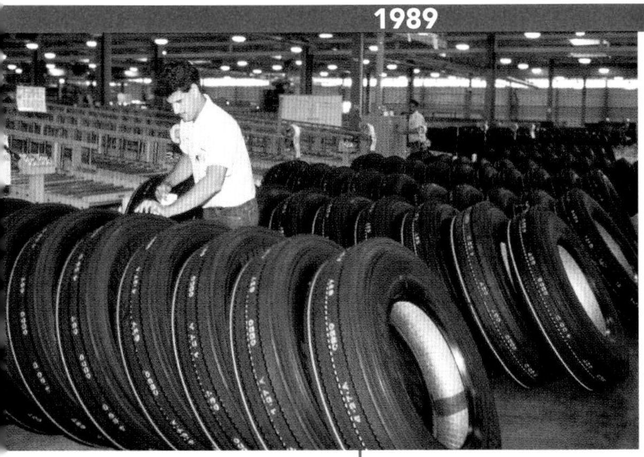

February 2 – Bridgestone Corporation announces it will build a $350 million truck tire plant in Warren County, Tennessee. Tire production begins in November 1990.

August 1 – Bridgestone Corporation of Japan announces plans to integrate Firestone, Bridgestone (U.S.A.) and Bridgestone (Canada) into a single corporation called Bridgestone/ Firestone, Inc., to be based in Akron, Ohio. The actual consolidation takes place in 1990. The Firestone operations in Latin America and New Zealand are later consolidated into Bridgestone/ Firestone, Inc.

November – Bridgestone Corporation announces a $1.5 billion capital investment program to increase productivity and improve quality within the Firestone plant network in the Americas.

December 31 – John Nevin retires from the company.

1990

August – The Wilson, North Carolina, plant becomes the first Firestone plant to produce Bridgestone brand passenger tires.

July – Bridgestone/ Firestone establishes 21 independent division companies. Each of these has a president who reports directly to the Bridgestone/ Firestone chairman and CEO. The purpose is to create bottom line accountability in the managers of the various businesses.

August – The long established Firestone rubber tree plantation in Liberia resumes operations following two years of civil strife in Liberia during which time all operations had stopped.

1993

May 14– In a ceremony just outside the Indianapolis Motor Speedway, Bridgestone/ Firestone announces its return to the Indianapolis 500 and Indy/Champ car competition. Firestone tires had not been in the competition for 20 years. U.E. "Pat" Patrick, one of the most respected team owners in racing history, and talented driver Scott Pruett became key partners in the race tire testing and development program. Pruett logs more than 12,000 miles in 1994 to help the Firestone Racing program prepare for the 1995 season.

1994

January – A new operating division, Bridgestone/ Firestone Off Road Tire Company, is formed to focus resources on the important Off the Road (OTR) tire market.

1995

May 28 – In its first Indianapolis 500 race in 20 years, Firestone-equipped drivers Scott Goodyear and Scott Pruett lead the race in the closing laps and are poised to make a one-two finish when mishaps occur. Pruett is involved in an accident and then a pacecar-passing penalty removes Goodyear. The impressive performance before the mishaps provides evidence that Firestone tires will win at the Brickyard in the near future.

1996

July 30– Scott Pruett produces the first "modern era" win for the Firestone Racing program when he drives the #20 Patrick Racing Lola/Ford to victory at the Michigan 500.

Bridgestone/Firestone announces it will expand its Akron Technical Center, creating 50 new jobs.

January 27 – The first-ever Indy Racing League event is contested at Walt Disney World Speedway in Florida and a Firestone-equipped driver is the first across the finish line. Buzz Calkins sets up a clean sweep of Firestone victories in the first year of IRL competition.

May 12– Arie Luyendyk, driving the Firestone-equipped Jonathan Byrd/Bryant Reynard Ford Cosworth, shatters the one- and four-lap qualification records at Indianapolis Motor Speedway. His best lap is 237.498 mph; his average for the four lap session is 236.986 mph.

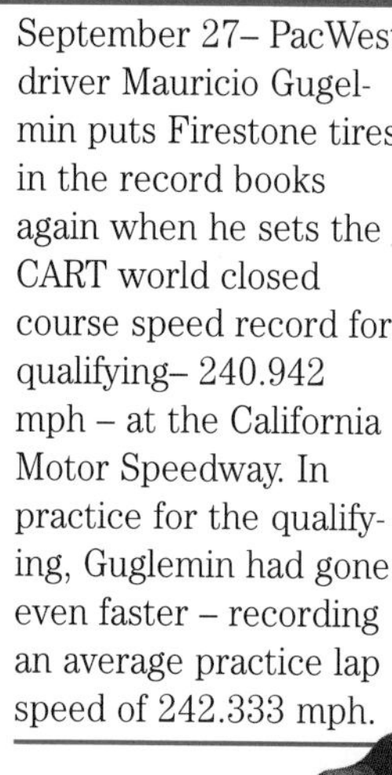

September 27– PacWest driver Mauricio Gugelmin puts Firestone tires in the record books again when he sets the CART world closed course speed record for qualifying– 240.942 mph – at the California Motor Speedway. In practice for the qualifying, Guglemin had gone even faster – recording an average practice lap speed of 242.333 mph.

1998

Dayton Tire becomes the title sponsor of the Indy Lights Championship racing series, the beginning of a long-term program to bolster the Dayton brand name with consumers.

May 7 – Bridgestone/ Firestone introduces its UNI-T AQ™ technology which combines UNI-T with two new technologies (Extended Performance Compound and Dual Layer Tread, known collectively as Extended Performance Optimization) that reduce the degradation in wet performance that can occur as the tire wears. Initially available in the Bridgestone Potenza S-02 Pole Position, UNI-T AQ was incorporated into the Bridgestone Turanza Revo and Bridgestone Dueler HL and HP tire lines in 1999.

August – Bridgestone/ Firestone introduces a run-flat tire, the Firestone Firehawk SH30® RFT, which does not require a special wheel.

1996

May 26 – The Firestone Racing program records its first Indianapolis 500 win of the modern era – and its 49th Brickyard victory overall – when Hemelgarn Racing driver Buddy Lazier, using Firestone tires, earns the right to have his likeness on the Borg-Warner trophy.

June – Bridgestone/Firestone introduces the Firestone Firehawk SZ50 with UNI-T,® a combination of advanced technologies involving tire design methods, construction and materials. A subsequent tire featuring UNI-T, the Firestone FT70c, later becomes one of the best selling tires in company history.

November – Bridgestone/Firestone and the USWA reach a tentative agreement to end the labor discord. Union members ratify the agreement the following month.

1997

May 27 – After being delayed two days due to rain, the 81st running of the Indianapolis 500 sees Arie Luyendyk – "the Flying Dutchman" – collect his second win at Indy, and the 50th for a Firestone-equipped driver. Luyendyk, driving for Treadway Racing, collected a purse of more than $1.5 million.

August 17 – The 1997 IRL season comes to a close with Robbie Buhl winning the Loudon 200 on Firestone tires. Tony Stewart, also on Firestone tires, claims the 1997 IRL driver's championship.

November 1 – Target/Chip Ganassi Racing driver Jimmy Vasser wins the CART season-ending race at Fontana, giving the Firestone Racing program an incredible record of 18 wins in 19 contests in the 1998 Championship Auto Racing Teams competition. Firestone drivers also collected 18 poles and – for the third consecutive year – the CART season championship went to the Firestone-equipped Target/Chip Ganassi Racing team and driver Alex Zanardi.

1999

The 1999 CART season comes to a close with Firestone-equipped drivers completely dominating the series. In the Indy Racing League, Texan Greg Ray, driving for Team Menard, won the IRL season championship. Goodyear withdraws from competition, making Firestone the sole tire for CART and IRL in 2000.

2000

January 29 – The 2000 racing season begins with Firestone driver Robbie Buhl winning the Indy Racing League season opener.

August 3 – It is now 100 years from the moment when the original Firestone Tire & Rubber Company was founded. It survives today and is a top global player as Bridgestone/Firestone, Inc., employing more than 45,000 in North and South America. BFS has become one of the world's largest tire manufacturers. Today it produces some 8,000 different tires for cars, trucks, buses, farm equipment and earth-moving equipment. Since the merger, it has invested more than $2 billion in new and upgraded facilities and sales have increased 65%. In addition to the Bridgestone and Firestone brands, BFS makes and markets Dayton, Sieberling, Road King, Gillette and Peerless brands. There are 17 tire plants as well as 22 facilities engaged in non-tire manufacturing. BFS is supported by six research and development centers and proving grounds.

Firestone in Victory Lane – A Remarkable Record

Each of Firestone's unprecedented 50 Indy wins has its own remarkable story. As a whole, they give testament to the consistency and performance of both the product and people.

1. **1911 - Ray Harroun** — The first annual Indianapolis 500 auto race is won in 6 hours, 42 minutes, and 8 seconds for an average speed of 74.59 miles per hour. The car is the famous Marmon Wasp equipped with a novel rear-view mirror, which Harroun uses to keep an eye on the other drivers.
2. **1913 - Jules Goux** — The first foreign-built car to be equipped with Firestone tires wins the day with the largest winning margin ever in an Indianapolis race—13 minutes, 8 and four-tenths seconds.

1917–1918 — First World War suspends the race.

3. **1920 - Gaston Chevrolet** — The first win on one set of natural rubber tires and the beginning of an amazing Firestone streak of Indy victories that will stretch through 1966 for 43 consecutive wins.
4. **1921 - Tommy Milton** — The ninth annual race is won with an average speed of 89.62 miles per hour.
5. **1922 - Jimmy Murphy** — Murphy is also the Indy car Champion for the year in all AAA events.
6. **1923 - Tommy Milton** — Milton is the first two-time winner of the 500. The buzz among the drivers was about the new Firestone "Gum-Dipped" tires which reduced their fears of blowouts.
7. **1924 - Joe Boyer/L. L. Corum** — The first Indy win with two drivers sharing credit.
8. **1925 - Peter DePaolo** — The balloon tire makes its Indy debut and DePaolo becomes the first winner to average more than 100 miles per hour.
9. **1926 - Frank Lockhart** — For this year only, the race is 400 and not 500 miles. The winner's average speed is 95.90 miles per hour.
10. **1927 - George Souders** — The winner of the annual Brickyard race averages 97.54 miles per hour.
11. **1928 - Louis Meyer** — For the first time, Meyer will end the year as AAA Indy car Champion. He will repeat the following year and again in 1933, when he takes both the 500 and the overall championship.
12. **1929 - Ray Keech** — The Indy referee is one of the race's greatest boosters, Harvey S. Firestone. Firestone broadcasts the event worldwide employing the greatest sportscaster of the day, Graham McNamee.
13. **1930 - Billy Arnold** — The record is set for the most laps led in an Indy 500 race by a single driver—198.
14. **1931 - Louis Schneider** — The win comes on the same day President Hoover asks the nation to remain steadfast in "this the Valley Forge of the Depression." The race is seen as a diversion from increasingly hard times.
15. **1932 - Fred Frame** — Frame races to victory in a Miller Hartz Special, averaging 104.1 miles per hour.
16. **1933 - Louis Meyer** — Meyer's second victory. This time his car averages 104.16 miles per hour.
17. **1934 - Bill Cummings** — Cummings outdistances the field at a blazing 104.9 miles per hour.
18. **1935 - Kelly Petillo** — A new track record is set at 106.24 miles per hour. Petillo tells Harvey S. Firestone, Sr., and his sons he could not have won without his Firestone tires.
19. **1936 - Louis Meyer** — The first three-time winner in Indy 500 history.

20. 1937 - Wilbur Shaw	A new speed record is set at 113 miles per hour in what is deemed to be the most glorious Indy win to date. Shaw prevails for the final 74 miles in the race, facing a combination of strong winds and a track temperature of 106 degrees. The brick and asphalt track begins to buckle and swell during the race. Roughly 175,000 very hot spectators cheer Shaw to victory.
21. 1938 - Floyd Roberts	The winner's average speed reaches 117.20 miles per hour.
22. 1939 - Wilbur Shaw	One of the most popular drivers ever, he is a rarity among drivers: a native of Indianapolis.
23. 1940 - Wilbur Shaw	Riding on Firestone tires, Shaw becomes the second triple winner of the Indy 500. This is the first win on synthetic tires. During the War, he will become the Firestone Aircraft Company's sales manager. In 1945, he will test Firestone synthetics for the company as its prime "test driver."
24. 1941 - Mauri Rose/Floyd Davis	Rose relieves Davis, who is running in 15th place, and wins the race. It is the second time in Indy history that two drivers share a car.
1942–44	The race is again suspended for a world at war. Firestone racing tire technology is key to a different kind of win—both the Army and Navy adopt racing construction for combat zone vehicles.
1945	The war is over but the Brickyard is overgrown and in need of repairs.
25. 1946 - George Robson	Three of Harvey S. Firestone's sons and two of Henry Ford's attend this race, which also serves to celebrate the Golden Anniversary of the Automobile Industry.
26. 1947 - Mauri Rose	On the way to his second Indy win, Rose sets a new track record of 116.338 miles per hour. Rose has ties to Akron; 20 years earlier, he was a popular local driver.
27. 1948 - Mauri Rose	In his 11th Indy appearance, Rose makes his third trip to Victory Lane to claim Firestone's 25th consecutive victory.
28. 1949 - Bill Holland	With Holland's win, Lou Moore becomes the only car owner ever to win three consecutive victories. In 1947 and 1948, he won with Mauri Rose.
29. 1950 - Johnnie Parsons	Raymond C. Firestone is on hand to congratulate Parsons on his new track record of 124.002 miles per hour.
30. 1951 - Lee Wallard	In a rain-shortened 345 mile race, the average speed sets a new track record, almost five miles per hour faster than the 1950 record. Later Wallard writes to Harvey S. Firestone, Jr., "This new track record would never have been possible except for the phenomenal performance of your new tire."
31. 1952 - Troy Ruttman	The youngest winner at age 22.
32. 1953 - Bill Vukovich, Sr.	It is 98 degrees in the shade, and with track temperatures at 130 degrees, the tires themselves are running hot—about 300 degrees. Vuky says of his tires after the race: "They stood up under the toughest conditions any tires have ever required."
33. 1954 - Bill Vukovich, Sr.	He wins, completing the course in a record 3 hours, 49 minutes, 17.27 seconds, with an average speed of 130.840 miles per hour. It is his second consecutive win. It is the first Indy 500 for Firestone tires made using nylon cord.
34. 1955 - Bob Sweikert	Swikert's win is overshadowed by tragedy. The popular Bill Vukovich, Sr., seeking his third consecutive win, is killed in a four-car crash.
35. 1956 - Pat Flaherty	In a telegram sent to Harvey S. Firestone, Jr., the 30-year old winner said: "Today I realized the dream of every race driver by winning the Indianapolis 500 at an average speed of 128.490 miles per hour...It was a great satisfaction to me, and I know it was for you, that the tires of champions proved once again to be the world's safest tire."

36. 1957 - Sam Hanks Another new record is set—135.601 miles per hour—and without a single tire problem. It is not only the fastest race in history but also the safest. The total absence of any tire problems shortens pit stops and yields record times. Hanks wins the Indianapolis 500 from his 12th start on Firestone tires, capturing the record for the most starts for a first-time winner.

37. 1958 - Jimmy Bryan Racers continue to whittle away at the time. Bryan of Phoenix, Arizona, completes the 500-mile course in 3 hours, 44 minutes.

38. 1959 - Rodger Ward Ward coasts onto Victory Lane after a blistering average speed of 135.857 miles per hour.

39. 1960 - Jim Rathmann The winner uses Firestone large-diameter, narrow-treaded tires.

40. 1961 - A. J. Foyt The postwar domination by Firestone is so strong that the first new tire brand to appear at the track in many years is a Dunlop. It finishes in ninth place.

41. 1962 - Rodger Ward A new average speed race record of 140.292 miles per hour is set before 230,000 spectators. Ward and his crew post a dazzling pit record: three stops for fuel and Firestone tires for a total time in the pits of 1 minute, 2.6 seconds.

42. 1963 - Parnelli Jones Another new speed record is set at 143.147 miles per hour.

43. 1964 - A. J. Foyt For the first time since 1920, the race is won on one set of tires from start to finish and once again they are a set of Firestones, this time, wide tires.

44. 1965 - Jim Clark The first win with a rear-engine car. Clark does what Gaston Chevrolet and A. J. Foyt, Jr., did before him—wins on one set of Firestones. He is the first to average more than 150 miles per hour.

45. 1966 - Graham Hill A rookie wins on Firestone tires at the 50th annual Indianapolis 500 auto race. Nearly half of the 33 starters were involved in a first-lap crash, but only one driver was hurt. Firestone's new fuel cells are credited with reducing the fire hazards of this accident-prone race.

46. 1969 - Mario Andretti A track average speed record is set at 156.867 miles per hour and one set of tires does it for the fourth time in Indy 500 history. All four cars completing the 500 on a single set of tires do so with a single brand—Firestone. Firestone's 46th win was hard to achieve. In 1967, Parnelli Jones was leading in the 197th of the 200 laps in the race when a six-dollar bearing failed, taking him out of the race with ten miles to go. In 1968, Firestone driver Joe Leonard had a wide and comfortable lead in lap 191 when his turbine engine blew.

47. 1970 - Al Unser, Sr. This and the next year's victories are won on Firestone's low-pressure, super-wide tires—some 16 inches across the tread of the rear tires.

48. 1971 - Al Unser, Sr. Unser joins Wilbur Shaw, Rodger Ward, A. J. Foyt, Bill Vukovich, Sr., as drivers with multiple Indianapolis 500 wins on Firestone tires. Air pressure in Unser's tires was approximately that of tires in the standard passenger car, 26 to 30 pounds per square inch of air in contrast to the 100 to 125 pounds per square inch in Ray Harroun's car in 1911.

49. 1996 - Buddy Lazier Firestone is back in the winner's circle for the first time in 25 years after an extended leave from motorsports competition. Lazier takes the checkered flag while riding on Firestone Firehawks.

50. 1997 - Arie Luyendyk The 50th driver to win on Firestone tires—a collective total unequaled by all other tire companies combined.

CHILDREN, GRANDCHILDREN AND GREAT-GRANDCHILDREN OF HARVEY S. FIRESTONE (1868-1938) / IDABELLE SMITH FIRESTONE (1874-1954)

Harvey Samuel Firestone, Jr. (1898 - 1973) /
Elizabeth Parke Firestone (1902 - 1990)

*Elizabeth Chambers Willis (1922 - 1989)**
Elizabeth Parke (Mrs. William) Leatherman (1956 -)

*Martha Parke (Mrs. William Clay) Ford (1925 -)**
Martha Parke (Mrs. Peter) Morse (1948 -)
Sheila Firestone (Mrs. Steven) Hamp (1951 -)
William Clay Ford, Jr. (1957 -)
Elizabeth Hudson (Mrs. Charles) Kontulis (1961 -)

*Harvey Samuel Firestone III (1930 - 1960)**
Diane Elizabeth Firestone (1958 -)

*Anne Idabelle (Mrs. John) Ball (1933 -)**
John Fleming Ball, Jr. (1959 -)
David Firestone Ball (1961 -)
Sheila Anne (Mrs. Randall) Burkert (1963 -)

Russell Allen Firestone (1901 - 1951) /
Dorothy Bryan Firestone (1901 - 1986)

*Russell Allen Firestone, Jr. (1926 -)**
Douglas Bryan Firestone (1950 -)
Andrew Phillip Firestone (1952 -)
Leigh Ann Firestone (1957 -)
Mark Alan Firestone (1963 -)
Russell Allen Firestone III

*David Morgan Firestone (1930 -)**
Amy Morgan (Mrs. Hart) Goodrich (1956 -)
David Morgan Firestone, Jr. (1958 -)
Jeffrey Bryan Firestone (1959 -)

Leonard Kimball Firestone (1907 - 1996) /
Polly Curtis Firestone (1909 - 1965)
Barbara Heatley Firestone (1915 - 1985)
Caroline Lynch Firestone (1926 -)

*Kimball Curtis Firestone (1933 -)**
Kimberly Jean Firestone (1961 - 1978)
Carey Greene (Mrs. Timothy) Romer (1962 -)
William Curtis Firestone (1964 -)
Leonard Lane Firestone (1966 -)
Christopher Kimball Firestone (1971 -)

*Anthony Brooks Firestone (1936 -)**
Catherine Hayley (Mrs. Douglas) Jessup (1960 -)
Adam Brooks Firestone (1962 -)
Polly Curtis (Mrs. David) Walker (1964 -)
Andrew Boulton Firestone (1975 -)

*Lendy Stewart (Mrs. Darrell) Brown (1939 -)**
Layton Leonard Register (1963 -)
Kyle Croft (Mrs. Peter) Swan (1964 -)

Raymond Christy Firestone (1908 - 1994) /
Laura An Lisk Firestone (1911 - 1960)
Jane Allen Firestone (1918 - 1994)

*Christy An (Mrs. Kenneth) Taucher (1936 -)**
Alison V. Gordon-Creed (1962 -)
Geoffrey Raymond Gordon-Creed (1963 -)

*Judith An (Mrs. Dale) Thiel (1939 -)**
Laura Fern (Mrs. Toby) Edwards (1964 -)
Charles Raymond Thiel (1971 -)

Roger Stanley Firestone (1912 - 1970) /
Mary Seagrave Davis Firestone (1915 - 1943)
Ann Joers Firestone (1923 - 1993)

*Gay Idabelle Firestone Wray (1938 -)**
Maryanne Haynes Wray (1959 -)
Laurie Davis Wray (1962 -)
Timothy Firestone Wray (1966 -)

*Peter Stanley Firestone (1940 - 1981)**
Nicholas Stanley Firestone (1966 -)
Lisa Scott Firestone (1967 -)

*John Davis Firestone (1943 -)**
Mary Cleaveland Firestone (1977 -)
Lucy Drummond Firestone (1979 -)

*Cinda Joers (Mrs. Manny) Fox (1948 -)**
William Roger Fox (1987 -)

*Susan Clark (Mrs. Daniel) Semegen (1955 -)**
Sarah Catherine Semegen (1984 -)
Mark Harvey Semegen (1986 -)

Elizabeth Idabelle Firestone (1914 - 1941) /
Ray Austin Graham, Jr. (1914 -)

*Ray Austin Graham III (1940 -)**
Gregory Morgan Graham (1972 -)

**Asterisks denote grandchildren of Harvey and Idabelle Firestone. Great-grandchildren are listed directly under their parents.*

CHAIRMEN

The Firestone Tire & Rubber Company

Harvey S. Firestone, Sr., 1932-1938
John W. Thomas, 1941-1946
Harvey S. Firestone, Jr., 1948-1966
Raymond C. Firestone, 1966-1976
Richard A. Riley, 1976-1981
John J. Nevin, 1981-1989

Bridgestone/Firestone, Inc.

George W. Aucott, 1990-1991
Yoichiro Kaizaki, 1991-1996
Masatoshi Ono, 1996-present

ACKNOWLEDGMENTS

A number of good people outside the immediate Bridgestone/Firestone family helped the authors in their search for ideas and images. In alphabetical order they are:

Joseph William Buff
American Highway Users Alliance, Washington, D.C.

Amy Dawson
Photo Archivist, Cleveland Public Library

Jack E. Gieck
a former product manager in the Industrial Products Division and
author of *Riding on Air: A History of Air Suspension,* published October 1999
by Society of Automotive Engineers Press

Andrea Klein and the staff
Bookseller Inc., old and rare books, in Akron

Lori L. Mavrigia
Managing Editor, *Modern Tire Dealer,* Akron

John V. Miller
Director of the Archive Services, the University of Akron

Steve Passion
Archivist, the University of Akron

The Staff of the Akron Public Library

Robert J. Ulrich
Senior Editor, *Modern Tire Dealer,* Akron

Kristen Utowitz
Tire Industry Safety Council, Washington

Russell A. Vitale
Photographer, Akron

Richard F. Weingroff
Federal Highway Administration of the U.S. Department of Transportation

BIBLIOGRAPHY

The history of the Firestone name and family is an important reflection of the 20th century and will, as its reputation continues to grow, extend into the new century. The authors of this work are the first to admit that there is more to the story and hope that others will study and write about the subject. With this in mind, we present our best sources, which we have taken the liberty of annotating.

Allen, Hugh. *Rubber's Home Town: The Real-Life Story of Akron.* Stratford House, N.Y., 1949.

Brauer, Norman. *There To Breathe The Beauty: The Camping Trips of Henry Ford, Thomas Edison, Harvey Firestone and John Burroughs.* Norman Brauer Publications, Dalton, Pa. 1995.

Burroughs, John. *Our Vacation Days of 1918.* (published privately.) An account of a camping trip through the Appalachians made by Henry Ford, Thomas Edison, Harvey Firestone, Harvey Firestone, Jr. and John Burroughs in August 1918. This is a very hard item to find; but copies exist in the Akron Public Library and the University of Akron Archives.

Firestone, Harvey Samuel. *Men and Rubber; the Story of Business.* In collaboration with Samuel Crowther. Doubleday. Page & Company, Garden City, N.Y., 1926

Firestone, Harvey S., Jr. *Man On The Move: The Story of Transportation.* G. P. Putnum's Sons, N.Y., 1967.

Firestone, Harvey S., Jr. *The Romance and Drama of the Rubber Industry.* Firestone Park, Akron, Ohio, 1933.

Radio talks delivered by Harvey S. Firestone, Jr., on the *Voice of Firestone* program over the National Broadcasting Company, September 1931 to September 1932. Firestone Tire & Rubber Co. Firestone Park, Akron, Ohio.

Firestone Tire & Rubber Co. *All Out for Victory.* Firestone Park, Akron, Ohio, no date but ca. 1943–44. This booklet was prepared to illustrate the wide scope of Firestone Tire & Rubber's activities during World War II. There are many photos illustrating the plant, parts of weapons made for the war effort, etc.

Firestone Tire & Rubber Co. *Firestone Twenty-Fifth Anniversary (1900–1925).* Firestone Park, Akron, Ohio, 1925.

Firestone Tire & Rubber Co. The *Firestone Non-Skid.* Periodical issued bi-weekly from 1915 to the 1980s. Firestone Park, Akron, Ohio. The issue of March 21, 1935, Volume XXIII, Number 2, is a tribute to Harvey S. Firestone.

Firestone Tire & Rubber Co. *Pioneer and Pacemaker: The Story of Firestone.* Firestone Park, Akron, Ohio.1950.

Firestone Tire & Rubber Co. *Rubber, Its History and Development.* Firestone Park, Akron, Ohio, 1922.

Lakeside Press, R. R. Donnelley & Sons Co. *Harvey S. Firestone,* 1868–1938, Chicago, 1938. A privately printed extended eulogy.

Lewis, Clarice Finley. *A History of Firestone Park.* Akron, Ohio distributed by the Summit County Historical Society, Firestone Park Citizens Council, 1986

Lief, Alfred. *Harvey Firestone: Free Man of Enterprise.* McGraw-Hill, New York, 1951.

Lief, Alfred. *The Firestone Story.* McGraw-Hill (Whittlesey House), New York, 1951.

Love, Steve and David Giffels. *Wheels of Fortune: The Story of Rubber In Akron.* The University of Akron Press, Akron, Ohio, 1999. Based on a series in the *Akron Beacon-Journal,* this is a history of the rise, fall and transformation of the rubber industry in Akron.

Newton, James. *Uncommon Friends.* Harcourt Brace Jovanovich, San Diego, 1987.

Steiner, Stewart B. *The Firestone Story Revisited (1900–1975).* Unpublished book length manuscript. This important document was created by a member of the staff as an update to Alfred Lief's *The Firestone Story* which told the story of the company from 1900–1950. There is a copy in the University of Akron Archives, which may be the only copy held publicly.

United States Congress House of Representatives, Committee on Interstate and Foreign Commerce. Subcommittee on Oversight and Investigations. *Safety of Firestone Steel-Belted Radial 500 Tires:* Hearings before the Subcommittee on Oversight and Investigations of the Committee on Interstate and Foreign Commerce, House of Representatives, Ninety-fifth Congress, second session. Washington: U.S. Govt. Print. Off., 1978. Full account of the hearings held May 19–July 10, 1978.

Weingroff, Richard F. *FWHA Day By Day: A Look at the Federal Highway Administration.* Washington, D.C., 1996.

Yates, Brock. *The Indianapolis 500: the story of the Motor Speedway—Revised Golden Anniversary Edition.* Harper & Brothers, N.Y., 1961.

Young, James C. *Harvey S. Firestone (1868–1938).* Privately printed by the Lakeside Press, R. R. Donnelly & Sons Company, Chicago, 1938. A compelling summary of the life of Firestone written by one of his greatest admirers. The book also contains a moving tribute by the Reverend Doctor Walter F. Tunks.

Young, James C. *Liberia Rediscovered.* Doubleday, Doran and Co., N.Y., 1934.

Young. James C. *School Days and Schoolmates of Harvey S. Firestone.* Privately printed, 1929. Descriptions and photos of Firestone's early life in Columbiana Co.

Note on Sources: Generally, the most important sources of material we used were the Akron Public Library, the Archives of the University of Akron, the Library of Congress, and the files of *Modern Tire Dealer* magazine.